First World War
and Army of Occupation
War Diary

France, Belgium and Germany

18 DIVISION
Headquarters, Branches and Services
Royal Army Veterinary Corps
Assistant Director Veterinary Services
26 July 1915 - 31 March 1919

WO95/2023/3

The Naval & Military Press Ltd
www.nmarchive.com
Published in association with The National Archives

Published by

The Naval & Military Press Ltd

Unit 10 Ridgewood Industrial Park,

Uckfield, East Sussex,

TN22 5QE England

Tel: +44 (0) 1825 749494

www.naval-military-press.com

www.nmarchive.com

This diary has been reprinted in facsimile from the original. Any imperfections are inevitably reproduced and the quality may fall short of modern type and cartographic standards.

Contents

War Diary	Buigny	23/11/1916	30/11/1916
War Diary	Buigny-St Maclou	02/12/1916	15/01/1917
War Diary	Hedauville	16/01/1917	28/01/1917
War Diary	Bouzincourt	28/01/1917	06/03/1917
War Diary	Gough Huts	07/03/1917	23/03/1917
War Diary	Steenbecque	25/03/1917	25/04/1917
War Diary	Pernes	26/04/1917	26/04/1917
War Diary	Habarcq	27/04/1917	27/04/1917
War Diary	Agny	28/04/1917	15/05/1917
War Diary	S 17a 8.4	16/05/1917	14/06/1917
War Diary	Couin	18/06/1917	30/06/1917
War Diary	Boisleux Au Mont	01/06/1917	16/06/1917
War Diary	Couin	17/06/1917	01/07/1917
War Diary	Doullens	03/07/1917	03/07/1917
War Diary	Steenvorde	04/07/1917	05/07/1917
War Diary	Reninghelst	07/07/1917	14/08/1917
War Diary	Lederzeele	15/08/1917	01/09/1917
War Diary	Esquelbec	03/09/1917	23/09/1917
War Diary	Poperinghe	24/09/1917	10/10/1917
War Diary	Border Camp	11/10/1917	20/10/1917
War Diary	Poperinghe	25/10/1917	27/10/1917
War Diary	Proven	30/10/1917	04/11/1917
War Diary	J Camp	05/11/1917	15/11/1917
War Diary	Elverdinghe	21/11/1917	12/12/1917
War Diary	Rousbrugge	18/12/1917	03/01/1918
War Diary	Elverdinghe	04/01/1918	27/01/1918
War Diary	Rousbrugge	01/02/1918	07/02/1918
War Diary	Salency	09/02/1918	16/02/1918
War Diary	Baboeuf	17/02/1918	24/02/1918
War Diary	Villequier-Aumont	27/02/1918	21/03/1918
War Diary	Baboeuf	22/03/1918	24/03/1918
War Diary	Dive-Le-Franc	25/03/1918	25/03/1918
War Diary	Pimprez	26/03/1918	26/03/1918
War Diary	Carlepont	27/03/1918	27/03/1918
War Diary	Audignicourt	28/03/1918	29/03/1918
War Diary	Choisy	30/03/1918	30/03/1918
War Diary	Arsy	31/03/1918	31/03/1918
Miscellaneous	Work Of Mobile Vety Sections Diary a Retirement		
War Diary	On The March	01/04/1918	03/04/1918
War Diary	Saleux	04/04/1918	16/04/1918
Miscellaneous	Manage and Clipping		
War Diary	Saleux	16/04/1918	26/04/1918
War Diary	Cavillon	27/04/1918	05/05/1918
War Diary	Montigny	06/05/1918	17/05/1918
War Diary	Mollens-Au Bois	25/05/1918	31/05/1918
Miscellaneous	Homes in M V S Establishment of		
War Diary	Molliens-Au-Bois	02/06/1918	13/07/1918
War Diary	Cavillon	16/07/1918	31/07/1918
War Diary	St Gratien	01/08/1918	11/08/1918
War Diary	Contay	12/08/1918	24/08/1918
War Diary	Warloy	25/08/1918	26/08/1918
War Diary	Henencourt	28/08/1918	31/08/1918
War Diary	Henencourt Chateau	02/09/1918	02/09/1918
War Diary	Caterpillar Wood	07/09/1918	18/09/1918
War Diary	Caterpillar Wood	25/09/1918	25/09/1918
War Diary	Combles	28/09/1918	28/09/1918

War Diary	Beaucourt Sur L'Hallue	04/10/1918	16/10/1918
War Diary	Ronssoy Wood	17/10/1918	17/10/1918
War Diary	Serain	19/10/1918	19/10/1918
War Diary	Maretz	20/10/1918	20/10/1918
War Diary	Le Cateau	24/10/1918	11/11/1918
War Diary	Serain	13/11/1918	25/11/1918
Heading	18th W-A 19/2 Herewith War Diary for Dec 1918		
War Diary	Serain	14/12/1918	14/12/1918
War Diary	Ligny	17/12/1918	31/03/1919
War Diary	Ligny	01/03/1919	31/03/1919

18DIVISION

A. D. V. S.

AUG 1915-MAR 1919

121/6753

18th Division

H.Q. 18th Div:

A.D.V.S.

Vol: I

August 15

Mar '19

2

Instructions regarding War Diaries and Intelligence Summaries are contained in F. S. Regs., Part II. and the Staff Manual respectively. Title Pages will be prepared in manuscript.

WAR DIARY
or
~~INTELLIGENCE SUMMARY~~
(Erase heading not required.)

Army Form C. 2118

Place	Date 1915	Hour	Summary of Events and Information	Remarks and references to Appendices
FLESSELLES	July 26 to 29		18 Division arriving in groups via Southampton, Havre and Amiens. Few horse casualties on the journey. D.H.Q. at FLESSELLES. Most units had some of their horses changed by the veterinary embarkation inspector at Southampton in some instances for very trivial reasons & the horses issued were in soft condition and suffered more from the effects of the journey than the more seasoned animals.	
			83 Bde RFA attached to 51 Division and took Lt Anderson AVC with them.	
			General idea of distribution of veterinary officers. One with Mobile Vety Section. One attached to each Bde of artillery and one attached to 18 Div Train ASC. Each Vety officer to take charge of the Bde area to which his artillery bde is attached. V.O. Div Train to be with it entirely. Owing to 83 Bde RFA leaving the division and ASC Coys being also detached to various Bdes this arrangement cannot work satisfactorily at present therefore V.O. i/c Train will look after the headquarter Coy with which he lives & any other units requiring attendance and for executive work any other ASC Coys will be in charge of the V.O. of the area to which they are attached.	
			FLESSELLES ADVS i/c D.H.Q. 18 Signal Coy RE and R Sussex Pioneers	
			" Capt Rouston OC Mobile Vety Section and i/c 2 Sections D.A.C at MONTON VILLERS and Div Cav Sq WARGNIES	
			" Lt Rowbotham 150 Coy ASC and 54 Inf Bde area (HQ NAOURS)	
			MIRVAUX Lt Gilbert 82 Bde RFA and 53 Inf Bde area.	
			COISY Lt Thompson 84 Bde RFA and 55 Inf Bde area.	
			VAUX Lt Ellsworth 85 Bde RFA	
	Aug. 1		Reported to DDVS 3rd Army at H.Q. BEAUQUESNE	
	" 2		84 Bde RFA went to join 5th Division. Lt Ellsworth takes over 55 Inf Bde area. Wrote to ADVS 51 Div asking him to arrange for Vety attendance for 53 Inf Bde when it joins his division. Inserted paras in Div orders giving instructions for notifying O.C. Mob Vet Sec of horses for evacuation & also how to deal with horses too sick to travel when units move (i/c maine as directed in GRO 534)	(3)
"	" 3		Telegram received from Army H.Q. directing Capt Rouston to proceed to ENGLAND to take up appointment of ADVS to 32 Div, to be relieved by Lt Keppell (S.R) - cancelled later.	

1875 Wt. W593/826 1,000,000 4/15 J.B.C. & A. A.D.S.S./Forms/C. 2118.

Instructions regarding War Diaries and Intelligence Summaries are contained in F. S. Regs., Part II. and the Staff Manual respectively. Title Pages will be prepared in manuscript.

WAR DIARY
or
~~INTELLIGENCE SUMMARY~~
(Erase heading not required.)

Army Form C. 2118

Place	Date 1915	Hour	Summary of Events and Information	Remarks and references to Appendices
FLESSELLES	Aug 4		Found case of psoroptic mange in A Bty 85 Bde & evacuated it to Mobile Vety Section. Thorough disinfection & daily Vety inspection ordered. Inspected battery & found other horses alright. Issued circular memo to all units with reference to sending sick horses to Mobile Vety Sec & procedure when left in billets & calling attention to Div order on the subject.	
"	5		Inspected [illegible] horses sent to Mob Vety Sec for evacuation from 150 Coy ASC & sent back 5 as not being suitable cases (i.e. being remount cases). Advised VO i/c that he must in future exercise more firmness and discretion.	
"	7		Weekly consolidated return contains ten deaths from pneumonia — these occurred mostly in horses issued at Southampton and Havre. Sporadic & due to effects of journey on these unseasoned animals.	
MONTIGNY	8		Division moved into fresh billeting area. H.Q. at Chateau MONTIGNY. Mobile Vety Sec, Div Cav Sq and 150 Coy ASC FRECHENCOURT. 82 Bde RFA BUSSY LES DAOURS. 85 Bde RFA and 2 Sections DAC BEAUCOURT. 5?? Inf Bde H.Q. BONNAY. 55 Inf Bde attached to 51 Div. Horse of 150 Coy ASC with psoroptic mange transferred to Mob Vety Sec for evacuation. Several horses left in old billets unable to travel. OC Mobile Vety Sec notified by units & will visit them & remove when fit to do so. Telegram received at D.H.Q. ordering Capt Ruston to proceed to ENGLAND to take up appointment of ADVS in 5th Army. Lt Rowbotham to take over Mobile Vety Sec and Lt [illegible] Williams to join to make up deficiency.	
"	9		Applied to AAQMG for motor to go and see DDVS with reference to putting Lt Gelbart in command of Mob Vety Sec instead of Lt Rowbotham as I consider him more experienced and suitable for the appointment having done 8 months war service and being a very capable officer. Interviewed DDVS who said he would obtain the necessary sanction from IGC. OC Mobile Vety Sec evacuated 10 sick horses to No 5 Base Hospital ABBEVILLE. Entrained them at MERICOURT.	7

1875 Wt. W593/826 1,000,000 4/15 J.B.C. & A. A.D.S.S./Forms/C. 2118.

Instructions regarding War Diaries and Intelligence Summaries are contained in F. S. Regs., Part II. and the Staff Manual respectively. Title Pages will be prepared in manuscript.

Army Form C. 2118

WAR DIARY
or
INTELLIGENCE SUMMARY
(Erase heading not required.)

Place	Date 1915	Hour	Summary of Events and Information	Remarks and references to Appendices
MONTIGNY	Aug 10		Inspected 150 Coy ASC & found one horse (issued at Havre) isolated for itchiness. Suspicious of sarcoptic mange and sent to Mob. Vety Sec for isolation and further observation.	
	11		Lt G.L. Williams reported his arrival & placed temporarily with ASC. Lt Rowbotham took over Mobile Vety Sec temporarily from Capt Rouston. Telegraphed to DDVS re permission to give command of Section to Lt Gelbart. Reply sanctioning same received at night. Two unit chests ~~and~~ 1 gallon Tobacco Solⁿ & 240 ammon. carb. bottles brought from Base by AVC Sergt who took sick horses down.	
	12		Capt Rouston left for ENGLAND. Issued unit chest to 185 Coy RE to replace one used up.	
	13		Interviewed all V.Os in my office re returns &c. Furnished reports to DDVS on number of deaths from Pneumonia and measures taken to prevent spread of mange. Posted Lt G.L. Williams to 82 Bde RFA vice Lt Gelbart. Lt Gelbart took over No 30 Mobile Vety Section & Lt Rowbotham resumed duty with 18 Div Train.	
	14		Inspected horses collected by M.V.S yesterday & advised which should go to the Base.	
	16		Visited by DDVS who requires list of AVC men employed in the Division — only the three L/Cpls with	
	17		the Infantry Bdes who are all good men & well worthy of promotion to sergeants. Told DDVS.	
	18		9 Sick horses evacuated to Base by Mobile Vety Section.	
HEILLY	19		HQ of Division moved to HEILLY	
	20		Visited 82 Bde & advised Lt Williams re disposal of sick horses when the unit moves.	
	22 to 25		Units of the Division moving at various times into fresh area to take over portion of the line between 51st & 5th Divns. 119 H Battery RGA joined the Division and for the present at BONNAY.	
			Veterinary duties arranged as under	
			ADVS HEILLY DHQ HQRE HQRA and 18 Signal Coy RE.	
			Lt Rowbotham BONNAY 150 Coy ASC at BONNAY 151 Coy + 14 Remount DAOURS 152 Coy RIBEMONT 153 Coy HEILLY also temporarily 54 Inf Bde TREUX – RIBEMONT, MERICOURT and DERNANCOURT. 119 H.B at BONNAY for a day or two.	5

1875 Wt. W593/826 1,000,000 4/15 J.B.C. & A. A.D.S.S./Forms/C. 2118.

Instructions regarding War Diaries and Intelligence Summaries are contained in F. S. Regs., Part II. and the Staff Manual respectively. Title Pages will be prepared in manuscript.

WAR DIARY

or

~~INTELLIGENCE SUMMARY~~

(Erase heading not required.)

Army Form C. 2118

Place	Date 1915	Hour	Summary of Events and Information	Remarks and references to Appendices
HEILLY	Aug 25		Lt Gilbert VILLE OC mobile Vety Sec also of all units at VILLE. Div Squad Cavalry. 56th Fd Ambulance and B & C Battery, 82 Bde also Q Bty RHA & AC at DERNANCOURT.	
			Lt Williams BRAY HQ & A & B Btys 82 Bde 53 Inf Bde, 1 Coy Sussex Pioneers 79 Fd Coy RE. adv dressing Stn 55 Fd Amb and 82/BAC at TREUX.	
			Lt Thompson MEAULTE 84 Bde RFA C/85 55 Inf Bde (less 1 Batt) R Sussex Pioneers (less 1 Coy) 55 Fd Amb adv DS 84 BAC at TREUX	
			Lt Ellsworth BONNAY HQ 85 Bde & A Bty. D.A.C 2 Sections. B/85 BUIRE and 85/BAC TREUX.	
			DAQMG 18 Div did not agree with this distribution saying that it should be arranged in areas and that it was absurd for one V.O. to have to ride four or five miles when there was another man in the area he was visiting. Worked out a distribution of areas with him as follows —	
			MEAULTE-DERNANCOURT area Lt Thompson. This includes 84 Bde RFA, C/85, 55 Inf Bde (less 1 Batt), 80 Fd Coy RE, Sussex Pioneers (less 1 Coy), 55 Fd Amb adv D Stn Q Bty RHA & AC, 119 H B RGA and 11 R Fusiliers.	
			BRAY area Lt Williams. A/82 B/82 53 Inf Bde 79 Fd Coy RE Sussex Pioneers (1 Coy) 55 Fd Amb adv D Stn	
			VILLE and TREUX area Lt Gilbert OC mob Vety Sec, Div Cav Squad, C/82, D/82, 56 Fd Amb 82/B.A.C 84/B.A.C 85/BAC (less 1 sec) HQ 54 Inf Bde and B/85 at BUIRE.	
			MERICOURT-RIBEMONT area Lt Rowbotham with 150 Coy ASC at BONNAY & 153 HEILLY. This area Mericourt-Ribemont includes 152 Coy ASC 7/Bedford Regt 6/Northants & 55 Fd Amb dressing Stn.	
			BONNAY-DAOUR area Lt Ellsworth, HQ 85 Bde RFA & A/85, D.A.C. 2 sections, 151 Coy ASC, 54 Fd Amb	
	26		On thinking this distribution out during the night I came to the conclusion that the O.C Mobile Vety section had too large a charge including his section, especially as there are several sick cases left behind when the troops moved which require visiting frequently. Drafted out a redistribution of these last three areas to make a	6

1875 Wt. W593/826 1,000,000 4/15 J.B.C. & A. A.D.S.S./Forms/C. 2118.

Instructions regarding War Diaries and Intelligence Summaries are contained in F. S. Regs., Part II. and the Staff Manual respectively. Title Pages will be prepared in manuscript.

WAR DIARY
or
~~INTELLIGENCE SUMMARY~~
(Erase heading not required.)

Army Form C. 2118

Place	Date 1915	Hour	Summary of Events and Information	Remarks and references to Appendices
HEILLY	Aug 26		more even division of work, as follows:–	
			Lt Gilland VILLE mobile vety sec, [illegible] Cav Squad, 56 Fd Amb ~~[illegible]~~ C/82 D/82 + B/85 at BUIRE	
			Lt Rowbotham BONNAY, to move to RIBEMONT and live with 152 Coy ASC instead of 150 Coy & to take the MERICOURT-RIBEMONT-TREUX area – 151 Coy ASC. HQ 54 Inf Bde. 7/Bedfords 6/Northants, 82/BAC 84/BAC 85/BAC (less 1 sec) and 153 Coy ASC at HEILLY	
			Lt Ellsworth BONNAY} 150 Coy ASC. HQ 85 Bde. A/85 · D.A.C 2 sections DAOURS} 151 Coy ASC. 54 Fd Ambulance.	
			Sent this to DAQMG who returned it saying the Div. order had already been drafted on the subject and that it was not considered advisable to alter it.	
			Appealed to the AA QMG who would not concur in moving Lt Rowbotham from the 150 Coy with which he had been living, although admitting that the amount given to OC mobile section was excessive. Neither would he agree to allowing Lt Rowbotham to do this area from BONNAY on the grounds that it was too far to go (distance from BONNAY to TREUX 4 miles). He said this might only be a temporary measure for a few days as other movements might be made. Told him I could not be responsible for the efficient performance of veterinary duties under these circumstances.	
	27		Motored to FRECHENCOURT and FLESSELLES to see horses which had been left in billets. Called at BEAUQUESNE on way back & discussed the occurrence of yesterday with DDVS who agreed with me that it was not a fair distribution and showed me other Divisions' distribution of officers in nearly all of which the OC MVS had no charge at all. DDVS will speak on the subject if I let him know that no alteration has been made in a few days.	✓
	28		Inspected 84/BAC & visited Ribemont, Treux, Ville & Mericourt. Visited Lt Thompson at MEAULTE.	

1875 Wt. W593/826 1,000,000 4/15 J.B.C. & A. A.D.S.S./Forms/C. 2118.

Instructions regarding War Diaries and Intelligence Summaries are contained in F. S. Regs., Part II. and the Staff Manual respectively. Title Pages will be prepared in manuscript.

WAR DIARY
or
INTELLIGENCE SUMMARY
(Erase heading not required.)

Army Form C. 2118

Place	Date	Hour	Summary of Events and Information	Remarks and references to Appendices
	1915			
HEILLY	Aug 29.		Weekly Returns to DDVS, percentage of sick less than 2% & these mostly injuries	
	" 30		Divisional Supply Officer tells me that a good many units do not indent for all the horse rations which it is possible to obtain so send extract for DO advising that full amount of forage should be drawn & recommending the extra 2 lbs of green forage when adequate grazing not available.	
	"		Applied to DAQMG for authority for Mobile Vety Sec to draw forage rations for 20 horses as a reserve store to cope with the arrival of several horses at the same time. Authority given & passed to OC M.V.S.	
	" 31		Wrote a private note to DDVS drawing his attention to the distribution of VO's in my last A2000 & informing him of the one proposed by me & cancelled by DAQMG & AAQMG. This moving of Vety Officers appears to me to come under the heading of administration of personnel and to be a technical matter to judge the amount of work which should be given to each officer, as the capabilities & capacity of each can only be properly appreciated by the head of the department to which they [illegible] belong.	
			11 Horses sent to Base by No 30 Mobile Vety Sec.	
			[illegible] Major AVC ADVS 18 Div	
				8

1875 Wt. W593/826 1,000,000 4/15 J.B.C. & A. A.D.S.S./Forms/C. 2118.

18th Division

121/6971

H.Q. 18th Division A.D.V.S.

Vol: II

Sep/. 15

ard

9

Instructions regarding War Diaries and Intelligence Summaries are contained in F. S. Regs., Part II. and the Staff Manual respectively. Title Pages will be prepared in manuscript.

WAR DIARY
or
~~INTELLIGENCE SUMMARY~~

(Erase heading not required.)

Army Form C. 2118

Place	Date 1915	Hour	Summary of Events and Information	Remarks and references to Appendices
HEILLY	Sept. 2		DDVS motored over to see DAQMG about distribution of Vety Officers. Both DAQMG & AAQMG out. Showed him No 4 Coy ASC (late 153) & DAC No 1 & 3 Sections. Hq 85 Bde & ABty moved today to VILLE taking Lt Ellsmith with them. This will cause a redistribution of vety work and relieve the OC MVS of some units.	
	" 3		Interviewed all VOs who brought their weekly A2000 to my office. This will be a good plan every week when possible as I can check & question them without wasting time. It has always been a difficult matter to get correct returns owing to the constant changes of units & Vety officers' charge.	
			Drafted new distribution of VOs for D.O., after consultation with DAQMG – Lts Thompson & Williams as before. Lt Rowbotham ~~[illegible]~~ BONNAY–DAOURS and ASC coys at HEILLY and RIBEMONT. Lt Gilbert, MVS, Div Cav, 56 Fd amb & C & D/82 at VILLE. Lt Ellsmith 85 Bde at VILLE and BUIRE and all units in TREUX – MERICOURT – RIBEMONT area except ASC. AAQMG thinks Lt Ellsmith might include the 2 Coys ASC at RIBEMONT in his area to save Lt Rowbotham the time taken up in riding there so agree to this as the other section of the DAC will shortly return from 51 Div to BONNAY. This gives Lt Ellsmith all troops in the TREUX – MERICOURT – RIBEMONT area.	
			The A & Q Branches are inclined to view the distribution of VOs from a mechanical and mathematical standpoint without taking into consideration individual capacity or reliability and have a very incorrect idea of the use & work done by the Mobile Vety Sec. This is probably due to the fact that they do not appreciate the amount of visiting ^horses left^ and "cleaning up"	10

Instructions regarding War Diaries and Intelligence Summaries are contained in F. S. Regs., Part II. and the Staff Manual respectively. Title Pages will be prepared in manuscript.

WAR DIARY
or
~~INTELLIGENCE SUMMARY~~
(Erase heading not required.)

Army Form C. 2118

Place	Date 1915	Hour	Summary of Events and Information	Remarks and references to Appendices
HEILLY	Sept 3.		that is done by the O.C. M.V.S after a move.	
"	" 6		Inspected Q. Bty R.H.A (attached) horses looking in excellent condition. Issued a letter to all V.O.s strongly advising the bandaging of all wounds in connection with feet & coronets in order to prevent soil contamination & infection with the Necrosis bacillus which is in my opinion the constant cause of severe sloughs leading to septic coronitis and quittors — also warned them verbally against allowing or encouraging indiscriminate poulticing of feet or heels as noncommissioned officers and dressers are apt to think that the hotter the application is the more efficacious it is. Supervision is also necessary in the preparation of disinfectant solutions for wounds the tendency being to make them too strong.	
	" 8		My one charger sick with pleurisy. I have been using the farrier's horse in addition to my own since we arrived in the country & find plenty of work for two horses either day, as the "pool" in the H.Q. motor cars ties one down to getting back at a certain hour and is uncertain. L/Cpls Coleman, Lander and Southall with the Infantry Bdes promoted to sergeants from Sept 3rd. and 20 AVC sergeants to join R A Bdes and D.A.C as soon as possible (Special Local Corps Order 29)	
"	" 9		Inspected horses at Mobile Veti Sec for evacuation to Base. Indent for drugs sent by N.C.O. A.V.C	
"	" 10		19 Horses evacuated by Mobile Vety Sec to No 5 Base Hospital. Wrote to D.D.V.S re getting a 2nd charger.	

1875 Wt. W593/826 1,000,000 4/15 J.B.C. & A. A.D.S.S./Forms/C. 2118.

Instructions regarding War Diaries and Intelligence Summaries are contained in F. S. Regs., Part II. and the Staff Manual respectively. Title Pages will be prepared in manuscript.

WAR DIARY

~~or~~

~~INTELLIGENCE SUMMARY~~

(Erase heading not required.)

Army Form C. 2118

Place	Date 1915	Hour	Summary of Events and Information	Remarks and references to Appendices
HEILLY	Sept 13		Inspected 54 Inf Bde 80 Fd Coy RE 119 H B 127 Fd Coy RE (attached) 84 Bde RFA 4/85 C/85 HQ 53 Inf Bde and Sussex Pioneers animals generally looking well in infantry but some of RA rather on light side	
"	" 14		Inspected A/82 B/82 D/83 2nd Cav ASC 79 RE and 53 Inf Bde at BRAY. Infantry transport generally looking well: RA might look better.	
	15.		Inspected 17 Horses at Mob Vet Sec for evacuation and reported to DDVS re size of nails in use in the Divn, no complaints from farriers of nails being too large.	
			Received telegram from DDVS asking if I recommended Lt E.E. [illegible] (SE) for promotion replied "Yes strongly recommend". He is by far the best officer I have in every way.	
	16.		17 Horses sent to No. 5 Vety hospital by No 30 M V S	
			AVC sergeants arriving to the RA + DAC in accordance with New War Establishments	
			Inspected No 1 Coy ASC & DAC – horses & mules looking well.	
	" 17		DDVS called re postings of AVC sergeants, some having gone to the wrong units. Under his directions drafted out a list for altering same.	
	" 18		Met DDR 3rd Army at BONNAY and accompanied him on his inspection of DAC remounts	
			No 30 Mobile Vety Section moved from VILLE to MERICOURT	
	" 20		Went to ALBERT and inspected 83 Bde RFA which has just returned from 51 Divn and picked out a few thin animals to go to the base as not likely to improve with the coming winter.	12
			82 Bde RFA and 53 Inf Bde moved from BRAY to MEAULTE which necessitates a slight re-arrangement of Vety duties. This constant moving makes it very difficult	

1875 Wt. W593/826 1,000,000 4/15 J.B.C. & A. A.D.S.S./Forms/C. 2118.

Instructions regarding War Diaries and Intelligence Summaries are contained in F. S. Regs., Part II. and the Staff Manual respectively. Title Pages will be prepared in manuscript.

Army Form C. 21[illegible]

WAR DIARY
~~or~~
~~INTELLIGENCE~~ SUMMARY
(Erase heading not required.)

Place	Date 1915	Hour	Summary of Events and Information	Remarks and references to Appendices
HEILLY	Sept 20.		to carry on the veterinary duties satisfactorily when worked in areas and I am beginning to feel sure that it is ~~more~~ better to keep each V.O. more or less permanently in charge of certain formations even if he has to ride some distance daily & overlap another V.O. The constant changing of half a Bde here & there makes it a matter of extreme difficulty to get weekly returns when the V.O. i/c is changed for two or three weeks running and it is more difficult to get the V.O. to take the same amount of interest in his charge.	
	22		Authority received from 10th Corps H.Q. for ADVS to have a second charger.	
	23		Inspected horses for evacuation collected at M.V.S. Have been confidentially warned that an advance is likely to take place & that all horses likely to be an encumbrance to mobility should be sent down to hospital.	
	24		43 Horses evacuated to Base by No 30 Mobile Vety Sec. The M.V.S. can now hire a float which is a very great convenience & enables us to move at once cases which cannot be properly treated in their lines.	
	25		The DAA&QMG, in my absence, ordered my clerk to do some typewriting for his office although he was engaged on my weekly returns. On my return I went to the DAA&QMG and told him I could not spare my clerk as he had my returns to do. He replied that my returns were of no importance when there was <u>war</u> work to be done and that I must understand this. I disagreed with his views saying that although I was only too pleased for my clerk to give a hand when he was not working for me, he could not use him when wanted by me.	13

Instructions regarding War Diaries and Intelligence Summaries are contained in F. S. Regs., Part II. and the Staff Manual respectively. Title Pages will be prepared in manuscript.

WAR DIARY
or
~~INTELLIGENCE SUMMARY~~

(Erase heading not required.)

Army Form C. 2118

Place	Date 1915	Hour	Summary of Events and Information	Remarks and references to Appendices
HEILLY	Sept. 26		After further discussion the DAAQMG gave me a written order to attend the office at 2.30 PM & interview the AA&QMG. Made the same statement to the AA&QMG who, to my surprise, upheld the DAAQMG although I pointed out that I was allowed a clerk in W.E. & considered his services were entirely at my disposal. I said I should have to represent the matter to my DDVS, who would call me up if my returns were delayed. As a matter of fact there was no urgent necessity for A" to want to use my clerk & I can see no justification whatever for the DAAQMG to interfere with my office at all.	
	" 27		Motored to Army HQ & saw the DDVS with reference to my clerk, who said he would call & see the AA&QMG on the first opportunity.	
	" 28		Inspected horses for evacuation to Base at M.V.S. – 15 horses evacuated. Visited OC 83 Bde RFA at Bellevue Farm ALBERT and consulted with him about Lt Anderson AVC his V.O. whose conduct has been unsatisfactory owing to a tendency to over indulge in alcoholic refreshment. Also interviewed Lt Anderson and advised and warned him of the probable consequences of not keeping himself under control.	
	" 29		One mange (psoroptic) case sent in to Mob Vety Sec from No. 3 Sec D.A.C. Fortunately this animal belongs to a S.S. Corporal & has been kept by himself for some time. How he caught it is difficult to trace.	
	" 30		Inspected No 3 Sec of the DAC – no other animals shew any suspicious symptoms.	14

[signature] Major,
A.D.V.S. 18th Div.

121.
7432

18th Division

L

H.Q. 18th Div: A.D.M.S.

Vol 3

Oct 15

15

Instructions regarding War Diaries and Intelligence Summaries are contained in F. S. Regs., Part II. and the Staff Manual respectively. Title Pages will be prepared in manuscript.

WAR DIARY
or
~~INTELLIGENCE SUMMARY~~
(Erase heading not required.)

Army Form C. 2118

Place	Date 1915	Hour	Summary of Events and Information	Remarks and references to Appendices
HEILLY	Oct. 1.		Under instructions from DDVS attended at COUIN to see Major HOBDAY give a demonstration on the intradermic test for Glanders on horses of 48 Division. If reliable, as stated by him, this is both neat & economical & has many advantages over the hypodermic method in dealing with a large number of horses under service conditions.	
..	.. 2		Interviewed RA Bde Commanders with reference to transfer of stud grooms &c to the AVC. Issued circ memo to VOs re treatment of p.c. feet (attached)	18 DIV No 283 (V)
..	.. 4		DDVS called during my absence and had an interview with AA & QMG with reference to the use of my clerk by his Office.	
..	.. 5		Received 2nd Charger from DDR 3rd Army.	
..	.. 6		Inspected 83 Bde RFA and picked out four horses to send to Base for debility.	
..	.. 7		24 Horses evacuated by Mob Vety Sec 30 cases of gangrenous ulcer have suddenly occurred at DERNANCOURT in C/85 which moved there recently from sheds at MEAULTE and have been standing in the open during the recent wet weather. The watering here is unsatisfactory & the horses have been standing in mud up to their fetlocks awaiting the completion of the brick standings in course of preparation. Reported this to AA & QMG & issued a memorandum on the subject to H.Q. of all units (attached). Inspected Battery & cases & advised as to treatment.	18 DIV No 310/V

16

Army Form C. 211

Instructions regarding War Diaries and Intelligence Summaries are contained in F. S. Regs., Part II. and the Staff Manual respectively. Title Pages will be prepared in manuscript.

WAR DIARY
or
INTELLIGENCE SUMMARY
(Erase heading not required.)

Place	Date 1915	Hour	Summary of Events and Information	Remarks and references to Appendices
HEILLY	Oct 7		Attended lecture by Div. Commander at BUIRE in which he mentioned the high percentage of Kicks and ropegalls in this Division during the last two weeks.	
"	" 8		Sent for by the Div Commander at 9.30 A.M. and asked by him what I had done towards stopping the Kicks and ropegalls, that he held me responsible & considered I had neglected my duty in not having taken action. I said I was always writing units and advising the Officers in charge of them (this I have been doing most conscientiously since I first joined the Div) He asked me if I had ever put anyone under arrest & seemed surprised when I answered in the negative & ordered me to make an inspection of the whole Division & report to the AA&QMG, who was present during my interview.	
			Weekly A2000 shews Kicks 43 Ropegalls 29. No doubt a large proportion of these are due to ignorance & carelessness and to not using a larger percentage of heel ropes. The majority of the junior officers & most of the men are inexperienced in the management of horses & the Veterinary staff has been pretty fully employed (shorthanded as it is) in dealing with the sick & injured, and a large proportion of my own time has been taken up in supervising my very inexperienced V.O.s who have not yet learnt to decide when a horse ought to be evacuated or remain under treatment with his unit.	

Instructions regarding War Diaries and Intelligence Summaries are contained in F. S. Regs., Part II. and the Staff Manual respectively. Title Pages will be prepared in manuscript.

WAR DIARY
or
~~INTELLIGENCE SUMMARY~~

(Erase heading not required.)

Army Form C. 2118

Place	Date 1915	Hour	Summary of Events and Information	Remarks and references to Appendices
HEILLY	Oct. 9.		Inspected 83 Bde RFA and A/85 attached. This Bde & A/85 have between them about half the kicks of the whole Division. Interviewed AA&QMG & sent him a written report of my inspection, keeping copy for myself. Pointed out shortage of nosebags & headropes – not using heelropes & bad watering arrangements &c. Visited DDVS at Army HQ. re transfer of F...S (stud grooms) to AVC. A2000 shows Kicks 45 Ropegalls 32. Higher than last week.	
	" 11		Inspected D.A.C. & Div Cav Squad & wrote report to AA&QMG. 18 horses evacuated to base by M.V. Vety Sec.	
	" 12		Inspected 82 Bde RFA B/85 C/85 and No 1 Coy ASC. Written report to AA&QMG. ASC horses looking well except a few recently returned to Train from other units where they have apparently received the usual treatment meted out to "loaned" horses.	
	" 13		Inspected 84 Bde RFA 119 HB RGA & 80 Fd Coy RE. Report to AA&QMG. 80 Fd Coy RE looking thin & ragged as if overworked.	
	14		Inspected 82, 84 & 85 B.A.C. – No 3 Sec Amn(?) Horse Transport and Norfolk Regt. Report to AA&QMG. No 2 & 3 Coys ASC. Kicks & Ropegalls shew slight decrease this week.	
	" 15		Inspected D HQ. HQRA, 18 Signal Co RE, R Fusiliers & Northants. Report to AA&QMG. Signal Coy horses have improved recently.	JL(?)

1875 Wt. W593/826 1,000,000 4/15 J.B.C. & A. A.D.S.S./Forms/C. 2118.

Instructions regarding War Diaries and Intelligence Summaries are contained in F. S. Regs., Part II. and the Staff Manual respectively. Title Pages will be prepared in manuscript.

WAR DIARY
or
~~INTELLIGENCE SUMMARY~~
(Erase heading not required.)

Army Form C. 2118.

Place	Date 1915	Hour	Summary of Events and Information	Remarks and references to Appendices
HEILLY	Feb 16		Inspected Queens, E Surrey, R W Kents, Buffs & Bedfords, 53 Fd Amb & 56 do. Report to AA & QMG. The Infantry look after their horses better than the RA & take much more interest in them.	
			Inspected 54 Fd Amb at DAOURS. Report to AA & QMG.	
"	17		Visited DDVS at 3rd Army H.Q. re Pharms transfers & AVC sergts.	
"	18.		Wrote in to AA & QMG advising that all horses in regular work should be clipped "trace" high. They have grown their coats very rapidly lately & Induce sweat profusely in their work. Horses coming in in the evening are never properly dry & it is impossible to get them so under the belly consequently they run a great risk of developing pneumonia.	
			Inspected 53 Inf Bde and part of 83 Bde RFA. Have a regular system of visiting the V.O. each day of the week & going round his units with him. In this way I see practically every horse in the division once a week.	
			Drugs arrived to Mob Vet Sec from No 1 AVC Base Store Depot. Only 40 bandages sent instead of 300 indented for. Bandages are very necessary to prevent treads & cracked heels from getting infected with the necrosis bacillus & other pyogenic organisms prevalent in the highly manured soil.	
"	" 20		30 Horses evacuated to Base by Mob. Vet. Sec.	
	21	"	Order issued for all horses doing regular work to be clipped "trace high".	
"	" 23		Return of Kicks down to 24 at minimum for the week & Rope galls 2. More heel ropes are in use & the percentage issued has been increased from 25% to 50%	19

1875 Wt. W593/826 1,000,000 4/15 J.B.C. & A. A.D.S.S./Forms/C. 2118.

Instructions regarding War Diaries and Intelligence Summaries are contained in F. S. Regs., Part II. and the Staff Manual respectively. Title Pages will be prepared in manuscript.

WAR DIARY
or
~~INTELLIGENCE~~ SUMMARY
(Erase heading not required.)

Army Form C. 2118.

Place	Date 1915	Hour	Summary of Events and Information	Remarks and references to Appendices
HEILLY	Oct 25		Met O.C. 83 Bde RFA and went round his brigade with him. Most of the horses stabled in ALBERT advised that the thin ones should be kept together get as much extra feed as possible & exercise together instead of going with the other horses.	
			Orders received to transfer No 1322 Sergt E.N. King AVC from B/82 to H.Q. 12 Corps.	
..	.. 27		Visited A/84 & C/84 to see thin horses, which have improved & are getting extra hay. One case of suspected mange (sarcoptic) in the Buffs transferred to Mob Vet Sec and one case of suspected mange (psoroptic) from 150 Coy ASC transferred to Mob Vet Sec.	
..	.. 30		Met DDVS 3rd Army & took him to see a few vicious & unsuitable horses which required casting. Total admissions of kicks for the week 15 & Ropegalls 2. This reduction is largely attributable to the use of more head ropes.	
	31			

[illegible] Major
ADVS – 18 Division

20

1875 Wt. W593/826 1,000,000 4/15 J.B.C. & A. A.D.S.S./Forms/C. 2118.

Subject:- Horses: Punctured Foot. 18/Div.No. 283 (V)

21

~~Lieutenant~~,

I have noticed recently cases of punctured foot in which the sole has been partially stripped.

Veterinary Officers should bear in mind that this is an extreme measure leading to a long spell of disability and exposing a large surface for septic infection.

An ordinary case of punctured foot if treated at once only requires proper drainage and disinfection and when this has been done the less horn removed the better under the existing circumstances.

Cases which require removal of any extent of sole or frog are obviously cases for evacuation to the base as early as possible.

[signature]

Major A.V.C.,
A. D. V. S., 18th Division.

D.H.Q.,
2nd October 1915.

Subject:- Disability. Horses. 18/Div.No. 310 (V)

22

Headquarters,

A very large percentage of cases of disability in horses is due to infected wounds on the lower extremities of the limbs. This is entirely due to soil contamination which, in this country, is particularly rich in the bacilli of necrosis.

The smallest wound in connection with the heels and coronets should be viewed with the utmost concern and reported as soon as possible to the Veterinary Officer.

Every endeavour should be made to cleanse and protect them from the soil.

Poultices and hot formentations should not be applied unless ordered by the Veterinary Officer.

D.H.Q.,
8th October 1915.

[signature]
Major A. V. C.,
A. D. V. S., 18th Division.

H.Q. 18th Div:
A.D.V.S.
vol: 4

121
7856

Nov 15

23

Instructions regarding War Diaries and Intelligence Summaries are contained in F. S. Regs., Part II. and the Staff Manual respectively. Title Pages will be prepared in manuscript.

WAR DIARY
~~or~~
INTELLIGENCE SUMMARY

(Erase heading not required.)

Army Form C. 2118

Place	Date	Hour	Summary of Events and Information	Remarks and references to Appendices
~~[illegible]~~ HEILLY	NOV. 1	–	11 Horses sent to Base by Mob Vet Sec including 2 Remount Cases cast by DDR.	
	" 2		B/82 from duty with 5 Div returned to 18 Div & billeted at MORLANCOURT. Horse lines in a stubble field which cuts up directly & is in a very muddy condition but apparently there is no more suitable place there being no grass round the village. Stables are being built against a bank just off the road.	
	" 5		Lieut. M. SPARROW AVC att HQ 29 Heavy Bde reported to me having come into the divisional area. This V.O. will be in charge of 119 H.B. RGA. 12th H.B. RGA and 2nd Canadian H.B. RGA. (Corps troops)	
	" 9		Under instructions from DDVS inspected 2nd Canadian H.B. RGA at BUIRE and forwarded report on cases of Ringworm remaining from a previous outbreak. Only 5 cases remaining & these nearly cured.	
	"		Lt Rowbotham [?] AVC proceeded to ENGLAND on eight days leave his duties being performed by me during his absence.	
	" 11		Inspected 12th H Battery at MERICOURT. Horse lines in a terrible condition owing to the rain & horses watering in the river. Reported on same to AA&QMG 18 Div.	24
			16 Horses evacuated to No 5 Base Vety Hospital by Mob Vet Sec.	

1875 Wt. W593/826 1,000,000 4/15 J.B.C. & A. A.D.S.S./Forms/C. 2118.

Instructions regarding War Diaries and Intelligence Summaries are contained in F. S. Regs., Part II. and the Staff Manual respectively. Title Pages will be prepared in manuscript.

WAR DIARY

~~or~~

~~INTELLIGENCE SUMMARY~~

(Erase heading not required.)

Army Form C. 2118

Place	Date	Hour	Summary of Events and Information	Remarks and references to Appendices
HEILLY	Nov 12		Interviewed Bde Major 55 Inf Bde re Smoke Helmets for horses & decided that 30 per Battalion & 10 for Bde H.Q. would be sufficient. Also 30 per Fd Coy RE and 30 for ASC.	
"	" 17		1 Case suspected mange in 82 BAC transferred to M.V.S. for evacuation. No other suspected cases but a few of the horses getting lousy.	
"	" 18		23 Horses sent to Base by Mob Vet Sec	
			Transfers of AVC sergts to units not having old type farriers on [illegible] (promoted stud grooms) carried out leaving three surplus AVC sergts in the Division. Notified DDVS of same. This posting of AVC sergts has been very erratic apparently because precise information as to where they were needed was not obtained before posting them. The majority of the sergts posted to this Division strike me as being keen, competent and good class men and I much appreciate the assistance they are able to give.	
"	19		Inspected B/82 Battery horses at MORLANCOURT. This battery has recently returned from doing duty with another Division & has had to stand in the open in a particularly bleak place whilst stables are being built. There are many thin horses. Sent a report to O.C. 82 Bde advising special treatment for these.	
"	" 20		Sent copy of A2000 to DHQ for transmission to X Corps H.Q. This will be rendered every week in future and is sanctioned by the DDVS, whom I first consulted.	25
"	23		Made a further inspection of B/82 & sent four horses to Mob Vet Sec for evacuation for debility.	

1875 Wt. W593/826 1,000,000 4/15 J.B.C. & A. A.D.S.S./Forms/C. 2118.

Instructions regarding War Diaries and Intelligence Summaries are contained in F. S. Regs., Part II. and the Staff Manual respectively. Title Pages will be prepared in manuscript.

Army Form C. 2118

WAR DIARY
~~or~~
~~INTELLIGENCE SUMMARY~~

(Erase heading not required.)

Place	Date	Hour	Summary of Events and Information	Remarks and references to Appendices
HEILLY	Nov. 25		13 Horses evacuated by Mob Vet Sec.	
	" 26		Met DDR at MERICOURT, who cast three horses for vice.	
			Mob Vet Sec had a narrow escape from bomb dropped by enemy aeroplane.	
"	" 27		Inspected 12 HB RGA. Horses have gone off in condition a lot since their arrival and picked out seven cases for evacn for debility. They have not been getting enough hay. Only ten pounds per horse is sent up to railhead and the extra is to be requisitioned locally. This is now becoming very difficult to do & even oat straw is not available in sufficient quantity. I have represented this to D.H.Q.	
			All clipping forbidden by 3rd Army.	
			Sent remarks on increase of debility and lice to DHQ with my A2000 & copy to DDVS.	
"	" 29		Drafted out a D.O. for [illegible] with reference to fast trotting of horses and work given to thin horses & those obviously losing condition. There is a general tendency when trotting to go at the "trot out", due largely to ignorance in the art of riding & driving & the want of knowledge of the capacity of horseflesh.	
			Received a microscope with [illegible] stains, in a leather case.	
			Roads very slippery first thing ~~and~~ necessitating the use of frost nails & cogs for the first time this winter.	
			10 sick and 3 remount cases evacuated by Mob Vety Section.	
	" 30		My clerk on leave to ENGLAND.	26
			Inspected B/82 with O.C. 82 Bde. Slight improvement in some of the thin horses which are now stabled & getting special attention.	
			[illegible] Major ADVS 18 Division	

Army Form C. 2118

Instructions regarding War Diaries and Intelligence Summaries are contained in F. S. Regs., Part II. and the Staff Manual respectively. Title Pages will be prepared in manuscript.

WAR DIARY
or
INTELLIGENCE SUMMARY
(Erase heading not required.)

Place	Date	Hour	Summary of Events and Information	Remarks and references to Appendices
HEILLY	Dec. 1		Took over vety charge of Div Cav Squad 56 FA & 91 FA (att) also 30 MVS temporarily for Capt [illegible] who proceeded to England on leave.	
			Met Lt Ellsworth (Vety 85 Bde HQ), who said he had had a horse of 85 BAC die during the night after being ill yesterday with a swollen neck and throat and was going to hold a post mortem – from his description of the symptoms I suspected the possibility of anthrax & went with him to view the carcase. This strengthened my suspicions & I had the carcase buried in lime in a suitable place, thorough disinfection carried out and a swab taken for microscopic examn. No post mortem made. Temperatures of other horses taken all normal. Infection probable from the forage. Two smears prepared & sent to OC No 5 Vety Hospital with a request to examine & report by telegram.	
	" 2		12 HB RGA left to join 5th Division also 28 H Bde HQ & with them Lt M. SPARROW AVC.	
	" 3		1st Highland Fife HB RGA joined the Division and wagon lines at MERICOURT and RIBEMONT. Lieut A.V. Nicholas AVC arrived with 8th H Bde & reported to me also 8th H Bde HQ at ALBERT.	
			Orders received from DDVS 3rd Army to transfer No 7689 Sergt L. MARTIN AVC (att C/82) to 111th Inf Bde 37 Div and No 3345 Sergt E.C. Stewart AVC (att D/84) to No 9 HB RGA 37 Div. No 34709 Sergt J.E. COURT C.A.V.C arrived for duty with 2 Can HB RGA from HAVRE. Wrote to DDVS pointing out that there were two surplus sergts AVC in 2 Can HB RGA.	
	" 4		Recd telegram from OC No 5 Vety Hospital that examn of smears from horse of 85 BAC showed positive anthrax. The slides only reached him today having been delayed in transit. Reported case of anthrax had occurred to AA & QMG verbally also CRA & in writing to DDVS and French Mission for notification to French authorities. This Section of BAC placed in working segregation and have special watering trough. Temperatures taken daily.	28

Instructions regarding War Diaries and Intelligence Summaries are contained in F. S. Regs., Part II. and the Staff Manual respectively. Title Pages will be prepared in manuscript.

WAR DIARY
or
INTELLIGENCE SUMMARY
(Erase heading not required.)

Army Form C. 2118

Place	Date	Hour	Summary of Events and Information	Remarks and references to Appendices
HEILLY	Dec 5		Visited TREUX and inspected all the horses of 85 BAC. Normal & healthy and this case was evidently due to a chance infection from forage, which is likely to occur at any time or place and very likely to be overlooked or not recognised by inexperienced vety officers. Impressed on Lt Ellsworth the importance of at once notifying me if he had anything suspicious in future.	
			Motored to 3rd Army Head Quarters & took my A2000 to D.D.V.S.	
"	6.		Rode to ALBERT to meet Lt ANDERSON who did not turn up. Learnt that he had had an accident when riding home on Saturday evening and was taken to 56 Fd Amb at MERICOURT and sent from there to No 5 Casualty Clearing Station for cuts and abrasions about head & face.	
			Inspected 83 Bde RFA & Berks & Norfolks & put Lt Williams in temporary charge vice Lt Anderson.	
			Telephoned to DDVS asking for another V.O. as soon as possible.	
"	7		Interviewed M.O. who informed me that Lt Anderson was under the influence of drink.	
			Visited No 5 CC & found Lt Anderson had been evacuated to the Base. Telephoned this information to DDVS telling him that this Officer was under the influence of drink which probably contributed to the accident that it was not the first time he had been so & asking him to prevent his return to this Division.	
"	9		Received sick report on Lt Anderson from RAMC & forwarded to DDVS 3rd Army with a confidential report on this officer stating that I had frequently advised & warned him against over indulgence in drink, that he was careless & unreliable in his work and not fit to be in charge of a unit.	29

1875 Wt. W593/826 1,000,000 4/15 J.B.C. & A. A.D.S.S./Forms/C. 2118.

Instructions regarding War Diaries and Intelligence Summaries are contained in F. S. Regs., Part II. and the Staff Manual respectively. Title Pages will be prepared in manuscript.

WAR DIARY
or
INTELLIGENCE SUMMARY
(Erase heading not required.)

Army Form C. 2118

Place	Date	Hour	Summary of Events and Information	Remarks and references to Appendices
HEILLY	Dec 10		Evacuated 11 sick horses to No 14 Vety Hospital.	
			Detailed Lt A V Nicholas AVC to take on charge of 2 Cav HB RGA and No 3 Sec Aux H.T so that he will be in charge of all Corps troops.	
			Indented on Ordnance for 85 Smoke Helmets for horses to replace those lost by 53 Inf Bde.	
	12		Visited V Bty RHA which has just joined the Division & is located at FRECHENCOURT	
	13		Detailed Lt SC ROWBOTHAM to take temporary charge of 53 Inf Bde when they move into rest billets at DAOURS.	
	16		Capt P.J. AUSTIN A.V.C. arrived for duty vice Lt ANDERSON	
			116 HB RGA arrived in divisional area & located at BUIRE	
			Half 2 Cav HB departed	
	17		Capt AUSTIN attached to 82 Bde RFA at ALBERT.	
			Instructions received from X Corps through HQ 18 Div that all horses in Division and all Corps & Army troops attached are to be subjected to the Mallein test by the intra dermic palpebral method. This is because horses sent to Base hospitals have developed glanders and one or two divisions have had outbreaks of the disease. So far I have not seen any suspicion of glanders in the horses of this division.	
	18		11 Horses evacuated to Base by Mob Vet Sec.	
			Heard casually that Lt Ellsmith had had a suspected case of Anthrax which he had not reported	30

Instructions regarding War Diaries and Intelligence Summaries are contained in F. S. Regs., Part II. and the Staff Manual respectively. Title Pages will be prepared in manuscript.

Army Form C. 2118

WAR DIARY
or
INTELLIGENCE SUMMARY
(Erase heading not required.)

Place	Date	Hour	Summary of Events and Information	Remarks and references to Appendices
HEILLY	Dec 18.		Telephoned to him in the evening & found he had buried a horse, which died rather suddenly in C/85, for a suspected case of Anthrax instead of reporting to me first. Reported same to DDVS.	
	.. 19		Inspected C/85 and horses in same shed as suspected case which might have been due to a lead lesion. Despatched blood smears to No 14 Base Vety Hospital.	
	.. 20		Received telegram from No 14 Vety Hospital saying smears negative. Wrote report to DDVS & explained to Lt Ellsworth the necessity of giving me the opportunity of deciding for him when he has an Anthrax case or one he imagines to be suspicious which might avoid needless alarms and correspondence. Motored to 3rd Army H.Q. in response to telegram from DDVS & fetched 2500 doses of mallein for intra dermic palpebral use – also 6 syringes.	
	.. 21		Busy arranging mallein programme for RA & giving V.O.s instructions & syringes. RA brigades to be done at twice, half each battery each time in order to interfere as little as possible with duty. Lt Ellsworth on leave to ENGLAND	
	.. 22		Half 83 Bde RFA malleined – 2 needles broken.	
	.. 23		Half 84 Bde RFA malleined – one syringe broken.	
	.. 24		Half 82 Bde RFA malleined also half 1 & 3 Sections DAC (one syringe broken) and half 84th Bde RGA. Inspected horses malleined yesterday. No reactions.	31

1875 Wt. W593/826 1,000,000 4/15 J.B.C. & A. A.D.S.S./Forms/C. 2118.

Instructions regarding War Diaries and Intelligence Summaries are contained in F. S. Regs., Part II. and the Staff Manual respectively. Title Pages will be prepared in manuscript.

WAR DIARY
or
INTELLIGENCE SUMMARY
(Erase heading not required.)

Army Form C. 2118

Place	Date	Hour	Summary of Events and Information	Remarks and references to Appendices
HEILLY	25		Inspected 84 Bde horses under mallein test & DAC horses.	
			Other half of 83 Bde RFA malleined.	
	26		Other half 84 Bde RFA malleined	
			Inspected 82 Bde horses under mallein test.	
			Wrote report to AA&QMG on condition of B/83 – not satisfactory. Want more supervision.	
	27		Other half 82 Bde RFA malleined also remainder of 1 & 3 Secs DAC	
			Inspected 83 Bde	
			26 Horses evacuated to Base by Mob Vet Sec	
	28		Inspected DAC horses undergoing mallein test also horses of 14 Res Pk	
			just joined Division & having been in contact with mange	
			Inspected 82 & 84 Bde horses undergoing mallein test.	
	29		Inspected 84 Bde horses malleined	
			Motored to 3rd Army H.Q. & fetched another 2500 doses mallein.	
	30		Arranged programme for malleining with Inf Bde H.Q., RA & RE, RAMC	
			McDonald returned from leave.	32

[illegible] Major
ADVS 18 Div

1875 Wt. W593/826 1,000,000 4/15 J.B.C. & A. A.D.S.S./Forms/C. 2118.

Army Form C. 2118

Instructions regarding War Diaries and Intelligence Summaries are contained in F. S. Regs., Part II. and the Staff Manual respectively. Title Pages will be prepared in manuscript.

WAR DIARY
or
~~INTELLIGENCE SUMMARY~~
(Erase heading not required.)

Place	Date	Hour	Summary of Events and Information	Remarks and references to Appendices
	1916			
HEILLY	JAN. 1		Busy day for all VOs malleining horses.	
			Inspected horses malleined yesterday	
	2		19 horses evacuated to Base by 30 Mob Vet Sec including 1 case of psoroptic mange from Suffolk Regt (parasite found)	
	3		Inspecting horses malleined on Saturday	
	4		Visited 150 Coy ASC and took scrapings from 2 horses with suspected mange. Parasite found & horses transferred to Mob Vet Sec and one horse suspected, 2 contacts isolated.	
			12 horses evacuated to Base by Mob Vet Sec	
			168 Bde RFA and 2 Btys 16a Bde joined 18 Div for instruction.	
	5		Inspected 151 & 152 Coy ASC horses and one horse suspected mange in 151 Coy	
			Inspected 153 Coy ASC & found two horses with mange. Scrapings taken for Examn.	
			Recd telegram from DDVS to mallein 14 Res Pk (No 3 Sec) immediately – arranged with VO Train to do this tomorrow morning.	
			Lt Williams on leave to England	
	6		Inspected 20 cases of gangrenous ulcer which had suddenly occurred in B/84	
			sent 2 horses 153 Coy ASC & one 151 ASC to Mob Vet Sec for mange	
	7		Visited ASC & HAC at BONNAY & took scrapings from greys & Roan in 150 Coy ASC	
			Visited No 3 Sec 14 Res Pk after mallein inject.	34

Instructions regarding War Diaries and Intelligence Summaries are contained in F. S. Regs., Part II. and the Staff Manual respectively. Title Pages will be prepared in manuscript.

WAR DIARY
or
INTELLIGENCE SUMMARY
(Erase heading not required.)

Army Form C. 2118

Place	Date 1916	Hour	Summary of Events and Information	Remarks and references to Appendices
HEILLY	Jany 7		Lt Ellsworth reported kicked by mule & unable to carry out his malleining – arranged for Capt Gelland & Lt Nicholas to carry it out tomorrow.	
			Reported verbally to A.A.&Q.M.G. 18 Div on bad condition of 116 H.T.B. horse lines also that horses of 32 Div were being taken into river for watering and that another [illegible] had reared in B/85 from [illegible] infection.	
			Wrote report to 18 Div Art on 116 H.T.B. horse lines & the necessity for moving same.	
"	" 8		Visited 2 M.G.s of 164 Bde at TREUX and reported to 18 Div Art that no V.O. had arrived in charge of 168 Bde.	
"	9		Chg of 150 Coy ASC gave reaction to mallein test in left eye. Both eyelids swollen & discharge from inner canthus	
"	" 10		Retested chg in right eyelid	
			Malleined 6 H.Q. horses & inspected horses malleined on Saturday.	
"	" 11		Chg gave complete reaction in right eye. Shews no clinical symptoms & in fair condition but very aged.	
			Malleined X Corps H.Q. & Signals at QUERRIER	35

1875 Wt. W593/826 1,000,000 4/15 J.B.C. & A. A.D.S.S./Forms/C. 2118.

Instructions regarding War Diaries and Intelligence Summaries are contained in F. S. Regs., Part II. and the Staff Manual respectively. Title Pages will be prepared in manuscript.

WAR DIARY
or
INTELLIGENCE SUMMARY

(Erase heading not required.)

Army Form C. 2118

Place	Date	Hour	Summary of Events and Information	Remarks and references to Appendices
	1916			
HEILLY	Jan 12		Inspected X Corps HQ & Signals mallein'd yesterday. Reported to DDVS on telephone re glanders reaction	
	" 13		Chcly No 423 tested with McFadyeans mallein. 22 horses evacuated to Base by mob Vet Sec & limber sent to ~~[illegible]~~ Base to be replaced by float from No 5 Vety Hospital. Retested in right eye horse No 321 of U Bty which had given a doubtful reaction.	
	" 14		ASC horse shews typical systemic & local reaction to Subcutaneous mallein test & inspected by DDVS. U Bty horse normal at 24 hours.	
	" 15		ASC horse destroyed & found to have glanders nodules in both lungs – no other lesions. Buried in lime. DDVS present. U Bty horse swollen in lower eyelid at 48 hours & considered doubtful – sent to mobile Vety section for further test by subcut method. Malleining of horses of 18 Div finished & mallein return despatched to DDVS. Total No of animals tested – Horses 5738 mules 1026. Result 1 Reaction 1 doubtful reaction. Lt Williams returned from leave	36

Army Form C. 2118

WAR DIARY
or
INTELLIGENCE SUMMARY
(Erase heading not required.)

Instructions regarding War Diaries and Intelligence Summaries are contained in F. S. Regs., Part II. and the Staff Manual respectively. Title Pages will be prepared in manuscript.

Place	Date	Hour	Summary of Events and Information	Remarks and references to Appendices
HEILLY	1916 Jan 16		ADVS on leave to ENGLAND. Capt. Gilbert officiating. Reported to DDVS my views on reducing Mob Vet Secs and only giving one per Corps. I think this would be most severely felt in all Divisions & increase largely the number of deaths and destructions (which are quite plentiful enough as it is). Personally I have found my Mobile Section of the greatest assistance especially in dealing with cases of contagious disease or suspected cases. When removed to the Section one knows exactly where they are & can inspect them more frequently. A good officer in charge of the Mob Sec is also a check on the inexperienced officers in charge of units, who seem to leave my Staff which are [illegible] not suitable cases for evacuation. I sincerely hope Mobile Sections will not be taken away from Divisions & would sooner their establishment were reduced.	
	" 25		ADVS returned from leave – nothing out of the ordinary has happened during his absence	
	" 26		Case of mange (psoroptic) transferred to MVS from 150 Coy ASC. No. 13920 Pte A. G. Arnold AVC joined for duty as clerk to ADVS, from No. 2 Vety Hospital	37

1875 Wt. W593/826 1,000,000 4/15 J.B.C. & A. A.D.S.S./Forms/C. 2118.

Army Form C. 2118

Instructions regarding War Diaries and Intelligence Summaries are contained in F. S. Regs., Part II. and the Staff Manual respectively. Title Pages will be prepared in manuscript.

WAR DIARY
or
INTELLIGENCE SUMMARY
(Erase heading not required.)

Place	Date	Hour	Summary of Events and Information	Remarks and references to Appendices
HB [illegible]	1916 Jan 27		Inspected horses for evacuation at MVS. 23 Evacuated to Base	
			Visited 152 Coy ASC & inspected horses & the two [illegible] with mange case of 152 Coy attached.	
	" 29		Attended DDR 3rd Army at his Casting inspection of Remount Cases.	
	" 30		Inspected 1/Highland Fife H.B. RGA horses and found twelve horses affected with mange & many more suspicious. These horses were recently clipped for lice and the V.O. i/c thought the condition of their skins was due to lice as he had taken several scrapings which were examined with negative results so did not report them to me as suspected mange cases. Took a scraping from one of the worst & found a Sarcoptic acarus. Informed DDVS by telephone & AA&QMG verbally.	
	" 31		DDVS came over & saw horses of 1/Highland Fife Bty. Evacuated 25 as mange and 7 as suspected. One badly affected & thin destroyed. Stables disinfected &c and 30 horses segregated as suspicious for immediate clipping. All are infested with lice & when clipped will show extensive areas of depilation which is probably caused by the continued presence of lice & very liable	38

1875 Wt. W593/826 1,000,000 4/15 J.B.C. & A. A.D.S.S./Forms/C. 2118.

WAR DIARY
or
~~INTELLIGENCE SUMMARY~~
(Erase heading not required.)

Army Form C. 2118

Instructions regarding War Diaries and Intelligence Summaries are contained in F. S. Regs., Part II. and the Staff Manual respectively. Title Pages will be prepared in manuscript.

Place	Date 1916	Hour	Summary of Events and Information	Remarks and references to Appendices
HEILLY	Jan 31		to mask a simultaneous infection with mange until the latter disease becomes well pronounced. I am very strongly of opinion that a general rule of clipping in September, throughout the whole Army, would do much to prevent the outbreaks of mange and also greatly improve the condition of horses in hard work. As it is now, the majority of unclipped horses are affected with lice by Xmas time & the only way of curing them is by clipping. The longer lice are allowed to exist the more extensive are the lesions produced, especially on fine skins, & when lice are present the symptom of itchiness is rendered valueless as regards diagnosing mange. The examination of skin scrapings takes up a lot of time and as a rule the sarcopt is not easily found. If horses were clipped in September they would be saved all the sweating which long coated horses endure during the autumn months & by the beginning of winter would have grown new coats which would have the advantage of being <u>clean</u> if it was thought desirable to keep them on. L. M. Verney Major A.D.V.S. 18 Div	39

40

A.D.M.S. 18th Div.

Vol 7

Army Form C. 2118

WAR DIARY
or
INTELLIGENCE SUMMARY
(Erase heading not required.)

Instructions regarding War Diaries and Intelligence Summaries are contained in F. S. Regs., Part II. and the Staff Manual respectively. Title Pages will be prepared in manuscript.

Place	Date 1916	Hour	Summary of Events and Information	Remarks and references to Appendices
HEILLY	Feb. 1		Visited 1/Highland Fife H.B. & took scrapings from 9 horses suspicious of mange. Spent rest of day & night examining same with negative results.	
			3rd Army Commander with DDVS inspected 1/Highland Fife B'ty horses.	
	2		Instructed by DDVS to evacuate all suspected cases. 2 horses floated into Mob Vet Sec at the Commandant's request both of which were only fit to be destroyed.	
			Psoroptic acari found in scraping from tail of grey mare 150 Coy ASC which had been in Mob Vet Sec under observation. Very few skin lesions evident & animal in bad condition.	
			Further scrapings examined from horses of 1/Highland Fife H.B. with negative results. Mange report to DDVS.	
	3		Visited suspected horses of 1/Highland Fife H.B. & decided to wait until more when clipped out before evacuating as suspected mange.	
			Horse sent to Mob Vet Sec from 6/2 West Lanc Fd Coy RE (TF) very badly blistered from ~~paraffin~~ applied to skin without V.O being consulted. Wrote report on same to CRE calling attention to recent DRO re same & sent copy to DDVS	41

1875 Wt. W593/826 1,000,000 4/15 J.B.C. & A. A.D.S.S./Forms/C. 2118.

Instructions regarding War Diaries and Intelligence Summaries are contained in F. S. Regs., Part II. and the Staff Manual respectively. Title Pages will be prepared in manuscript.

WAR DIARY
or
INTELLIGENCE SUMMARY
(Erase heading not required.)

Army Form C. 2118

Place	Date 1916	Hour	Summary of Events and Information	Remarks and references to Appendices
HEILLY	Feb 3.		Cbly from A/82 sent to Mob Vet Sec with all hair off head neck & very itchy. looks like an acute case of sarcoptic mange & V.O. says he rubbed it all off in one night. Mule from Norfolk Regt also sent to Mob Vet Sec with hair rubbed off head neck & back but this animal is very full of lice which is probably the only cause of the irritation as scraping sent immediately & no parasites found.	
RIBEMONT	Feb 5		D.H.Q. moved today to RIBEMONT, also Mob Vet Sec. Lt Thompson returned from leave. Sent out orders to V.O's re charge of units when moves completed – Capt Gelbart 30 Mob Vet Sec also 1/c 150 & 151 Coy ASC & 135 Coy RE RIBEMONT. Capt Williams 82 Bde RFA BRESLE and Mob Sec 3rd Bridging Train RE also temporary charge (whilst Lt Rowbotham on leave) of D.A.C., 152 Coy ASC, Div Cav Squad and 1 Batt 55 Inf Bde at PONTNOYELLES. Lieut Thompson 84 Bde HQ D/84 & D/85 MEAULTE. HQ 55 Inf Bde MOULIN DU VIVIER 92 Fd Coy RE, Sussex Pioneers, Buffs & E Surreys DERNANCOURT 55 Fd Amb VILLE. Queens, 83 & 84 BAC & A B & C Btys 84 Bde BUIRE. Lt Ellmuth 85 Bde HQ, C/85, 85 BAC at LAVIEVILLE	42

1875 Wt. W593/826 1,000,000 4/15 J.B.C. & A. A.D.S.S./Forms/C. 2118.

Army Form C. 2118

Instructions regarding War Diaries and Intelligence Summaries are contained in F. S. Regs., Part II. and the Staff Manual respectively. Title Pages will be prepared in manuscript.

WAR DIARY
or
~~INTELLIGENCE SUMMARY~~

(Erase heading not required.)

Place	Date 1916	Hour	Summary of Events and Information	Remarks and references to Appendices
RIBEMONT	Feb 5.		[illegible]. 2 Batts 54 Inf Bde + 54 Fd Amb FRANVILLERS 2 Batts 54 Inf Bde + HQ LAHOUSSOYE	
"	" 6		Lt Rushton on leave to England.	
"	" 7		Piebald pony of 18 Signal Coy RE died suddenly last night without any apparent previous illness – considered the carcase rather abnormally decomposed for such a short-time dead so took blood smears from ear and sent to No 14 VH by Special DRLS for exam.	
"	" 8		4 Sick + 11 Remount cases evacuated by Mob Vet Sec. Received telegram from No 14 VH saying blood smears sent yesterday were so full of what appeared to be putrefactive bacilli that it was impossible to say whether anthrax or not but advising all precautions to be taken. Therefore buried carcase of pony deeply in lime + no P.M. made. Rather a peculiar case as blood from the ear should have been quite fresh had animal died from heart disease or from any non specific cause. All other horses in the Coy normal.	43

1875 Wt. W593/826 1,000,000 4/15 J.B.C. & A. A.D.S.S./Forms/C. 2118.

Instructions regarding War Diaries and Intelligence Summaries are contained in F. S. Regs., Part II. and the Staff Manual respectively. Title Pages will be prepared in manuscript.

WAR DIARY
or
INTELLIGENCE SUMMARY
(*Erase heading not required.*)

Army Form C. 2118

Place	Date 1916	Hour	Summary of Events and Information	Remarks and references to Appendices
RIBEMONT	Feb 10.		Recd letter from ~~DDVS~~ forwarding enclosure from DVS re horse of A/83 evacuated for mange and destroyed at Base by V.O. of the hospital who wrote saying he ~~had~~ was a bad case of sarcoptic mange & so generally miserable with a nasal discharge as well that he destroyed him & made a careful post mortem but didn't discover any glanders. DVS asks who was the V.O. responsible for allowing him to get into this condition. Called on Capt Williams for a written report & attached same with covering minute saying I had inspected the horse when he arrived in the Mob Vet Sec & considered him worth sending down also that I diagnosed the case as an acute infection of psoroptic mange & that the V.O's statement that the horse had rubbed himself into this condition in a single night was possible as I had seen it happen before. He had no nasal discharge when he left the M.V. Section.	
	" 11		Visited 1/Highland Fife H.B. & 116 H.B. & 119 H.B. Clipping of 1/Highland Fife proceeding & all horses full of lice & itchy.	
	" 12		83 Bde turned out of their stables in ALBERT. Sent [illegible] state of B/83 to ADVS 55 Div to which this Battn is now attached. Visited DAC at PONT NOYELLE. Horses in a very soft & muddy field with very little room to change the lines.	
	" 13		Inspected 1/Highland Fife H.B.	44

1875 Wt. W593/826 1,000,000 4/15 J.B.C. & A. A.D.S.S./Forms/C. 2118.

Army Form C. 2118

Instructions regarding War Diaries and Intelligence Summaries are contained in F. S. Regs., Part II. and the Staff Manual respectively. Title Pages will be prepared in manuscript.

WAR DIARY
or
INTELLIGENCE SUMMARY

(Erase heading not required.)

Place	Date 1916	Hour	Summary of Events and Information	Remarks and references to Appendices
RIBEMONT	Feb 14		16 Sick horses evacuated to Base including one case suspected Mange (Remount) from 119 H.B. Visited ALBERT. C/D/83 in very bad lines in a muddy & manure infected field likely to cause much trouble from gangrenous ulceration	
"	" 15		Visited 83 Bde at BRESLE, standings bad & approached through deep mud. Drew 4 electric torches from Ordnance for V.O.s to examine nostrils for glanders lesions. 39 Horses & 41 mules of 2/2 West Lancs Fd Coy RE (T.F.) malleined by intra dermic palpebral method temporarily attached to the Division.	
"	" 16		Interviewed Staff Captain RA re RA horse standings now that they have had to vacate the ones they had made during the winter and warned him of the dangers of soil infection of heels & coronets.	
"	" 17		Interviewed OC 85 Bde RFA re horse lines of 85 BAC being on a manure infected field & suggesting they might be moved to better ground, he did not agree that manured soil was harmful. Wrote report to C.R.A. re this matter. VBG AC horse in Mob Vet Sec retested with hypodermic mallein after a month from first test & again gave a doubtful reaction. Report to DDVS.	
"	" 18		Lieut Rowbotham granted an extension of leave till March 6. on M.C.	
"	" 19		Visited 1/Highland Fife HB & examined 11 horses for suspected mange. Took further scrapings.	45

Instructions regarding War Diaries and Intelligence Summaries are contained in F. S. Regs., Part II. and the Staff Manual respectively. Title Pages will be prepared in manuscript.

WAR DIARY
~~or~~
~~INTELLIGENCE SUMMARY~~
(Erase heading not required.)

Army Form C. 2118

Place	Date 1916	Hour	Summary of Events and Information	Remarks and references to Appendices
RIBEMONT	Feb. 20		Visited Army HQ & ~~[illegible]~~ had interview with the DDVS — asked him to try & get me another V.O. in place of Lt Rowbotham as owing to the extended area of the Division at present it is hard to carry on with one man short for more than a short period.	
			Visited DAC & wrote report to AA&QMG on condition of horse lines and necessity of moving same immediately if possible.	
			3 Machine Gun Sections have ~~just~~ recently joined the Division, one to each Bde. Each section has 52 animals & all are more or less mangy.	
..	.. 22		Inspected 1/Highland Fife H.B. & took scrapings from grey pony, very itchy.	
			12 sick horses evacuated to Base.	
..	.. 24		Sharp frost & snow roads very slippery.	
..	.. 25		Sarcoptes found in the pony of 1 Highland Fife HB. Evacuated him and 17 others for suspected mange. Healthy horses being dressed with Calcium Sulphide Soln.	
	.. 27		Inspected DAC horse sent into MVVS for suspected mange & took scrapings.	
	.. 28		Sarcoptes found in scraping from DAC horse — small patch of skin eruption on near shoulder.	46

1875 Wt. W593/826 1,000,000 4/15 J.B.C. & A. A.D.S.S./Forms/C. 2118.

Instructions regarding War Diaries and Intelligence Summaries are contained in F. S. Regs., Part II. and the Staff Manual respectively. Title Pages will be prepared in manuscript.

WAR DIARY

or

~~INTELLIGENCE SUMMARY~~

(Erase heading not required.)

Army Form C. 2118

Place	Date 1916	Hour	Summary of Events and Information	Remarks and references to Appendices
RIBEMONT	Feb. 29		Inspected horses of 1/1 Highland Fife H.B. & picked out 10 suspicious of mange. Further scrapings taken from and Sarcoptic again found in Nos 1721 & 1542. The former has already been scraped at least 6 times with negative results which shews how difficult it is to find the Sarcopt. in some cases. This battery is likely to shortly move to another area & I shall have all the horses dressed over with Calcium sulphide soln after examining these ten. Have carefully inspected the remainder & find none suspicious of mange but it will be necessary for V.O. to make regular & constant inspections whenever possible owing to the insidious nature of this form of skin disease.	
			[illegible] Major A.D.V.S. 18 Div	47

1875 Wt. W593/826 1,000,000 4/15 J.B.C. & A. A.D.S.S./Forms/C. 2118.

48

ADVS
19th DW
Vol 8

51

ADVS
18 DW
Vol 9 ~~8~~

Instructions regarding War Diaries and Intelligence Summaries are contained in F. S. Regs., Part II. and the Staff Manual respectively. Title Pages will be prepared in manuscript.

WAR DIARY

~~xx~~ of A.D.V.S.,
~~INTELLIGENCE SUMMARY~~ 19th Division.

(Erase heading not required.)

Army Form C. 2118

Place	Date 1916.	Hour	Summary of Events and Information	Remarks and references to Appendices
LA GORGUE.	March			
	1.		On leave. Capt. H. Bone, A.V.C., Acting A.D.V.S.	Fasu.
	2.		-do- -do- -do-	Fasu.
	3.		-do- -do- -do-	Fasu.
	4.		Returned from leave.	Fasu.
	5.		Routine work and inspected M.V.S.	Fasu.
	6.		Routine work and inspected 19th Signal Coy. and D.H.Q.	Fasu.
	7.		Inspections. Reported deficiency of one A.V.C. Sergeant with D.A.C. to replace No. 88217, F.Q.M.S. Underwood, evacuated.	Fasu.
	8.		Inspected D/86th Brigade, R.F.A. and A/86th Brigade R.F.A.	Fasu.
	9.		Inspected 5th South Wales Borderers. Took over Veterinary charge of 106th Inf. Bde. and No. 4 Coy. A.S.C. (35th Division).	Fasu.
	10.		All Veterinary Officers reported at Office.	Fasu.
	11.		Inspections and routine work.	Fasu.
	12.		To AIRE to see D.D.V.S., First Army.	Fasu.
	13.		Inspected 87th Brigade Ammunition Column, R.F.A.	Fasu.
	14.		Inspected Divisional Train, A.S.C., and A/88th Brigade, R.F.A.	Fasu.
	15.		Inspected 86th Brigade Ammunition Column, R.F.A.	Fasu.
	16.		Inspected 255th Tunnelling Company, R.E.	Fasu.
	[illegible]			

49

1875 Wt. W593/826 1,000,000 4/15 J.B.C. & A. A.D.S.S./Forms/C. 2118.

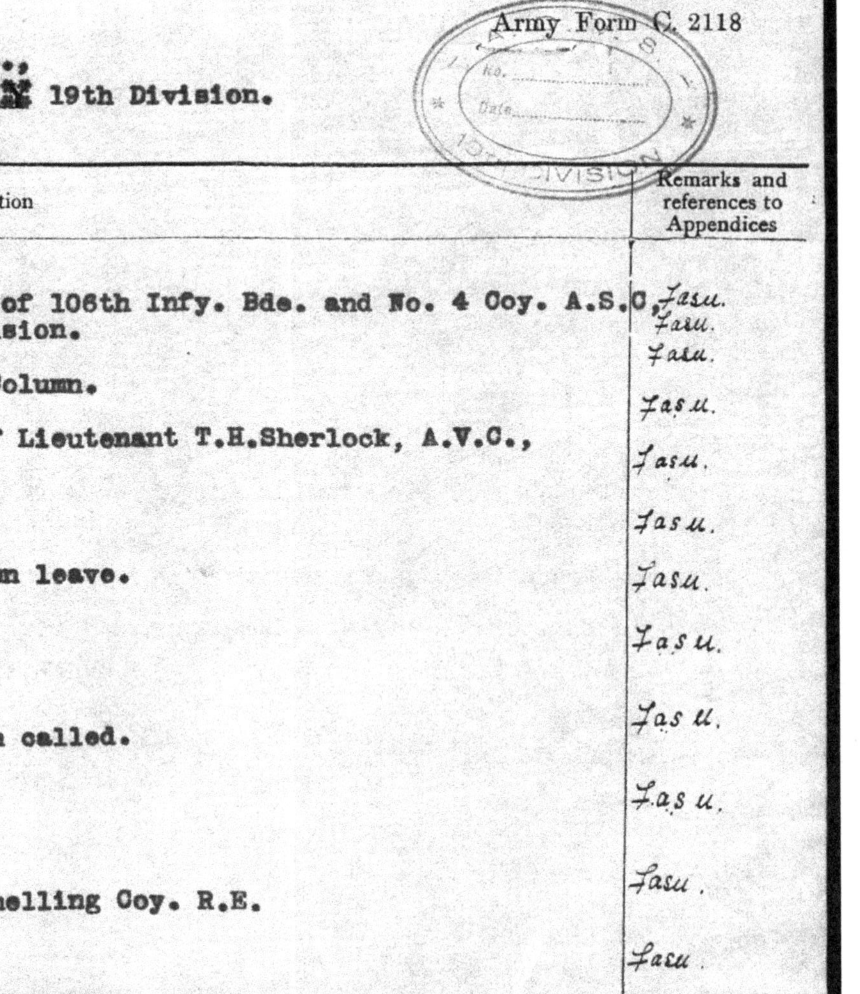

Army Form C. 2118

WAR DIARY

of A.D.V.S.,
~~INTELLIGENCE SUMMARY~~ 19th Division.

(Erase heading not required.)

Instructions regarding War Diaries and Intelligence Summaries are contained in F. S. Regs., Part II. and the Staff Manual respectively. Title Pages will be prepared in manuscript.

Place	Date 1916.	Hour	Summary of Events and Information	Remarks and references to Appendices
LA GORGUE.	March 17.		All Veterinary Officers reported. Forwarded A.F. A 2000 of 106th Infy. Bde. and No. 4 Coy. A.S.C. to A.D.V.S., 35th Division, these units leaving this Division.	Jasu. Jasu. Jasu.
	18.		Inspected 7/East Lancs. Regt. and Divisional Ammunition Column.	Jasu.
	19.		Routine work. Forwarded to D.D.V.S., second agreement of Lieutenant T.H.Sherlock, A.V.C., recommended for re-engagement.	Jasu.
	20.		Inspected D.A.C.	Jasu.
	21.		Routine work. Captain H. Bone, A.V.C., left for Englandsn leave.	Jasu.
	22.		Inspected Divisional Signal Company.	Jasu.
	23.		Inspected Divisional Train.	
	24.		All Veterinary Officers reported. A.D.V.S., 8th Division called.	Jasu.
	25.		Inspected 81st and 94th Field Coys. R.E.	Jasu.
	26.		Routine work and inspected M.V.S.	
	27.		Inspected 57th Brigade Machine Gun Section and 255th Tunnelling Coy. R.E.	Jasu.
	28.		Routine work and inspections of various units.	Jasu.
	29.		Inspected 19th Signal Company, D/86th Bde. R.F.A., and A/88th Bde. R.F.A.	Jasu.
	30.		Inspected 87th Brigade Ammunition Column, B/86th Bde. R.F.A., A/86th Brigade, R.F.A.	Jasu.
	31.		All ~~Vets~~ Veterinary Officers reported.	Jasu.
			**********	
			The weather during the early part of the month was cold, with snow and rain; during the middle of the month, unsettled; the latter part much warmer and generally clear.	J A S Moore Major AVC A.D.V.S. 19 Division

50

1875 Wt. W593/826 1,000,000 4/15 J.B.C. & A. A.D.S.S./Forms/C. 2118.

Instructions regarding War Diaries and Intelligence Summaries are contained in F. S. Regs., Part II. and the Staff Manual respectively. Title Pages will be prepared in manuscript.

WAR DIARY
or
INTELLIGENCE SUMMARY
(Erase heading not required.)

Army Form C. 2118

Place	Date	Hour	Summary of Events and Information	Remarks and references to Appendices
RIBEMONT	1916 March 2		18 Div in XIII Corps, Fourth Army from present date. DDVS Lt Col F.W. Hunt CAVC, HQ QUERRIER.	
	" 4		31 sick evacuated including 1 case suspected mange. Weather very severe.	
	" 6		DHQ moved to MONTIGNY. 54 Inf Bde and 152 Coy ASC attached to 30 Div temporarily.	
MONTIGNY	" 7		Distribution of VOs in new area as follows – Major Verney i/c DHQ & 18 Signal Coy RE MONTIGNY	
			Capt Gellatt 30 Mob Vet Sec MONTIGNY also i/c 151 & 153 Coys ASC BEHENCOURT and Div Cav Squad BRESLE	
			Capt Austin 83 Bde RFA & HQRA and 150 Coy ASC DAOURS	
			Capt Williams 82 Bde RFA at LA NEUVILLE, 79 Field Coy RE and 53 FA CORBIE, 53 Inf Bde & 54 FA LA HOUSSOYE and FRANVILLERS	
			Lieut Thompson 84 Bde RFA DAOURS 92 Fd Coy RE FRECHENCOURT, 55 Inf Bde & 56 FA. ST GRATIEN and ALLONVILLE	
			Lieut Ellsworth 85 Bde RFA and DAC at BUSSY LES DAOURS.	
	" 8		Visited Army H.Q. and called to see DDVS.	
	" 10		Lieut Ellsworth accompanied following units to BOIS DE TAILLES (30 Div area) A/82 B/83 D/83 C/84 A/85 C/85 D/85 85 BAC	
			Capt Austin taking over DAC and 85 Bde HQ remaining at BUSSY LES DAOURS.	
			Lieut Rowbotham not returned from sick leave. Wrote to DDVS asking for a relief as have now been short of one VO for 5 weeks.	
	" 11		10 Horses, left at DAOURS by other Divisions, collected by No 30 Mob Vet Sec.	
	" 13		Visited RFA at DAOURS. Horses in open & weather warm & dry. They are able to lie down & should benefit greatly from the weather & surroundings after having been crowded in brick standings for the last four months. Many are shockingly lousy and it is very difficult to get them clipped quickly enough in spite of a D.R.O. issued to the effect that "all horses affected with lice are to be clipped as soon as possible".	
			18 sick evacuated by 30 MVS including one suspected mange.	
	" 14		Lieut J BRADLEY AVC (TC) joined for duty vice Lt S.C. Rowbotham (sick) – attached to 18 Div Train ASC.	53

1875 Wt. W593/826 1,000,000 4/15 J.B.C. & A. A.D.S.S./Forms/C. 2118.

Instructions regarding War Diaries and Intelligence Summaries are contained in F. S. Regs., Part II. and the Staff Manual respectively. Title Pages will be prepared in manuscript.

WAR DIARY
or
INTELLIGENCE SUMMARY
(Erase heading not required.)

Army Form C. 2118

Place	Date 1916	Hour	Summary of Events and Information	Remarks and references to Appendices
ETINEHEM	Mar 20		Div HQ moved to ETINEHEM the 18 Div taking over the area from 30 Div	
			No 30 Mob Vet Sec moved to RIBEMONT (railhead)	
			Capt Austin i/c 83 Bde RFA BRAY and BOIS DE TAILLES, 54 Inf Bde and 80 Fd Coy RE BRAY.	
			Capt Williams i/c 82 Bde RFA, 53 Inf Bde, 79 Fd Coy RE 1 Batt 90 Inf Bde & 7 [illegible] Batt. Round Bray & Bois de Tailles.	
			Lt Thompson i/c 84 Bde RFA, 55 Inf Bde, 92 Coy RE & R Sussex Pioneers. Bray, Bois de Tailles & Suzanne.	
			Lt Bradley i/c 18 Div Train ETINEHEM and SAILLY LAURETTE. DAC 55 FA 56 FA 90 Bde HQ & [illegible] Sq at CHIPILLY 54 FA SAILLY LAURETTE and 2/R Fus ETINEHEM. Attachment: 9 Res Pk ASC.	
			Lt Spencer i/c 29 H Bde RGA and 1/2 [illegible] H B RGA BRAY and ETINEHEM CHIPILLY Rd 174 & 183 TC RE & 202 Fd Coy RE. 2 Batts 90 Inf Bde BRAY	
			Lt Ellsworth i/c 85 Bde RFA Bois de Tailles.	
			Lt Adams i/c 30 Div units remaining in this area B/148 D/148 & BAC. D/149 B/150 A/38 /151 & BAC XX Cable Sec RE	
	" 23		Lieut Ellsworth to ENGLAND on termination of his year's engagement. Capt Williams i/c 85 Bde RFA until relief arrives.	
	" 26		Lieut T O'CONNOR AVC (T.C) arrived in relief of Lt Ellsworth & is attached to 85 Bde RFA.	
			Many cases of gangrenous ulceration in horses of 29 H Bde & float has been busy since one arrived in this area, not many standings built & where there are standings the approach to same through deep mud.	
	" 28		Sarcoptic mange found in horses of 53 [illegible] Coy & 9 Res Pk sent to MVS as suspected cases. The latter had only joined from Remounts a week ago & was clipped on account of lice.	52
			[illegible] Verney Major ADVS. 18 Div	

1875 Wt. W593/826 1,000,000 4/15 J.B.C. & A. A.D.S.S./Forms/C. 2118.

Instructions regarding War Diaries and Intelligence Summaries are contained in F. S. Regs., Part II. and the Staff Manual respectively. Title Pages will be prepared in manuscript.

WAR DIARY or INTELLIGENCE SUMMARY

(Erase heading not required.)

Army Form C. 2118

ADVS 18 Div Vol 10

Place	Date 1916	Hour	Summary of Events and Information	Remarks and references to Appendices
ETINEHEM	Apl. 1		Telegraphed weekly state of Sick to DDVS. This is to be the rule in future.	
			No 4652 Sergt A. G. RIDDIFORD AVC joined C/85 to replace casualty.	
..	.. 2.		Inspected 12 HB RGA & found many horses in a lousy & debilitated condition. Advised general clipping & sent five cases to MVS for debility.	
..	.. 4		Notice a falling off in condition in all the RA horses especially those which have been in the Bois de Tailles. A good deal of this is due to difficulty in watering the horses having to go 1½ to 2 miles to the river & many are watered in buckets which is always unsatisfactory. The RE are going to lay water on into the wood & put up troughs but this will not be completed for some time.	
			Divisional Commander thinks it's too late in the season for general clipping & issued an order prohibiting it except under veterinary advice.	
			35 Sick evacuated.	
	.. 7		Wrote in to AA&QMG re clipping of lousy horses in No 2 Sec DAC which has not proceeded as fast as possible or necessary. Am quite convinced that lousiness has a great influence on loss of condition & debility owing to horses badly affected never getting any rest apart from the effect on the skin. Owing to the various contradictory orders which have been issued from time to time re clipping it is difficult to always get it carried out without delay even when urgently necessary for veterinary reasons.	54

1875 Wt. W593/826 1,000,000 4/15 J.B.C. & A. A.D.S.S./Forms/C. 2118.

Instructions regarding War Diaries and Intelligence Summaries are contained in F. S. Regs., Part II. and the Staff Manual respectively. Title Pages will be prepared in manuscript.

WAR DIARY
or
~~INTELLIGENCE SUMMARY~~
(Erase heading not required.)

Army Form C. 2118

Place	Date 1916	Hour	Summary of Events and Information	Remarks and references to Appendices
ETINEHEM	Apl 8		31 sick evacuated	
..	.. 10		DDVS visited me & inspected C/85 Bty which has many thin horses. Received complaint from OC No 1 Base Vety Stores of excessive indent for unit chests for this Div ~~since~~ last week – forwarded through DVS. Wrote & explained that nearly half the number indented for were for 30 Div units temporarily attached to 18 Div & for Corps & Army Troops. Shall in future send attached units indents to ADVS of their Division.	
..	.. 11		Sarcopt found on horse of 53 MG Coy which showed very slight skin lesions.	
..	.. 12		25 sick evacuated.	
..	.. 15		Wrote in to D.H.Q re number of cases of debility & quittor occurring in this unit's A2000 & sent copy of my remarks & suggestions to DDVS for information. Weather conditions are very severe but Officers i/c of Wagonlines do not take sufficient notice of horses losing condition and they are frequently missed by the V.O. as they are out at work when he makes his visits. It is necessary for officers in charge of wagon lines to make certain that these kind of horses are seen by the V.O. so that his advice may prevent the stage of debility being reached. Ignorance of horses & the capacity of horseflesh for work has a good deal to do with this omission and is often the reason horses are not evacuated earlier than is now the case. The V.O. often has a large area to cover & cannot time his visits to find all horses in more than very occasionally.	55

1875 Wt. W593/826 1,000,000 4/15 J.B.C. & A. A.D.S.S./Forms/C. 2118.

Instructions regarding War Diaries and Intelligence Summaries are contained in F. S. Regs., Part II. and the Staff Manual respectively. Title Pages will be prepared in manuscript.

WAR DIARY ~~or~~ INTELLIGENCE SUMMARY

(Erase heading not required.)

Army Form C. 2118

Place	Date 1916	Hour	Summary of Events and Information	Remarks and references to Appendices
ETINEHEM	Apl. 18		At the request of DAQMG visited railhead and issued 58 Remounts for 18 Div – Some of the H.D. were in very poor condition.	
	" 19		38 Sick evacuated.	
			6 horses of B/82 killed by a shell exploding under the team	
	" 21		Received Circular memo. from DVS re horses not being evacuated to Base early enough for chances of successful treatment & also the uselessness of evacuating hopeless cases. I do not think this Div has sinned much in sending down hopeless cases as the OC MVS & myself always consult over anything at all doubtful & never evacuate a case of open joint unless we think it has a fair chance of recovery. Occasionally, horses which are obviously useless for work from chronic foot lameness, but in good bodily condition, are sent to the Base as we know they can be sold to the butcher at the Base more easily & for double the price it is possible to get at the front. Although the ADVS can greatly assist, the sending down of cases early enough must always primarily depend on the Executive V.O.s & the judging of this is the most difficult thing inexperienced and temporary officers have to contend with.	
			Held a conference of all V.O.s in office, showed them the circular from DVS. & emphasized the necessity of finding out & sending to M.V.S. all cases of debility & quittor as early as possible.	56

Army Form C. 2118

Instructions regarding War Diaries and Intelligence Summaries are contained in F. S. Regs., Part II. and the Staff Manual respectively. Title Pages will be prepared in manuscript.

WAR DIARY
~~or~~
~~INTELLIGENCE SUMMARY~~
(Erase heading not required.)

Place	Date 1916	Hour	Summary of Events and Information	Remarks and references to Appendices
ETINEHEM	Apl. 23		40 Sick evacuated and one foal.	
"	" 24		Inspected C/149 just arrived into this area. Horses very poor.	
"	" 25		Reported verbally to Staff Capt RA. the poor condition of B/151 & C/149 Btys.	
			Capt Newton AVC returned from leave to England.	

C M Venney Major
ADVS. 18 Div

57

A.D.V.S. 19 Div

Army Form C. 2118

Vol 9

Instructions regarding War Diaries and Intelligence Summaries are contained in F. S. Regs., Part II. and the Staff Manual respectively. Title Pages will be prepared in manuscript.

WAR DIARY
of A.D.V.S.,
~~INTELLIGENCE SUMMARY~~ 19th Division.
(Erase heading not required.)

Place	Date 1916.	Hour	Summary of Events and Information	Remarks and references to Appendices
	May.			Fasu.
NORRENT FONTES.	1.		Evacuated 44 Aminals to Base Hospital. Inspected 86th Bde. R.F.A.	Fasu.
	2.		Evacuated 38 animals. Routine work.	Fasu.
	3.		A.D.V.S., 38th Division called. Routine work.	Fasu.
	4.		Evacuated 13 animals. Routine work.	Fasu.
	5.		Weekly conference of Veterinary Officers. To AIRE to see D.D.V.S.	Fasu.
	6.		Inspected 82nd Field Coy. R.E.	Fasu.
	7.		D.H.Q. moved to FLESSELLES. Office at No. Rue d'Eustache, FLESSELLES.	Fasu.
FLESSELLES	8.		Inspected 6th Wilts. and No. 3 Section Fourth Army Aux. H.T. Inspected site for Mobile Veterinary Section at ST VAST.	Fasu.
	9.		Took over veterinary charge of Section Fourth Army A.H.T. Coy. at VIGNACOURT. Mobile Veterinary Section moved to ST. VAST.	Fasu.
	10.		D.D.V.S., Fourth Army called. Routine work.	Fasu.
	11.		Inspected 82nd Field Coy. R.E.	Fasu.
	12.		Weekly conference of Veterinary Officers. Routine work.	Fasu.
	13.		Inspections and routine work.	Fasu.
	14.		Inspected 19th Divisional Train.	Fasu.
	15.		All Officers' veterinary chests inspected at M.V.S. Inspected Signal Coy. Section at H.Q. R.A., at BELLOY.	58

1875 Wt. W593/826 1,000,000 4/15 J.B.C. & A. A.D.S.S./Forms/C. 2118.

Army Form C. 2118

Instructions regarding War Diaries and Intelligence Summaries are contained in F. S. Regs., Part II. and the Staff Manual respectively. Title Pages will be prepared in manuscript.

WAR DIARY
of A.D.V.S.,
INTELLIGENCE SUMMARY 19th Division.

(Erase heading not required.)

Place	Date 1916.	Hour	Summary of Events and Information	Remarks and references to Appendices
FLESSELLES	May			Jasu.
	16.		Inspected 19th Divl. Signal Company.	Jasu.
	17.		Inspected 19th Divl. Signal Company.	Jasu.
	18.		Inspected 57th Infantry Brigade.	Jasu.
	19.		Weekly conference of Veterinary Officers. Captain Sherlock left on leave.	Jasu.
	20.		Inspected D.A.C.	Jasu.
	21.		Routine work. Inspected M.V.S. and D.H.Q.	Jasu.
	22.		Took over veterinary charge of one troop III Corps Cavalry Regiment. Inspected 58th Infy. Bde.	Jasu.
	23.		Inspected 56th Infantry Brigade.	Jasu.
	24.		Inspected D.A.C.	Jasu.
	25.		Inspected 58th Field Ambulance and 154 Coy. A.S.C.	Jasu.
	26.		Weekly conference of Veterinary Officers. Evacuated 48 animals.	Jasu
	27.		Inspected M.V.S. Routine work.	Jasu.
	28.		Inspected units at VIGNACOURT.	Jasu.
	29.		57th and 58th Infy. Bdes. left for training area, also 88th Bde. R.F.A. Inspected 86th and 87th Bdes. R.F.A.	Jasu.
	30.		Routine work. Inspected M.V.S.	Jasu.
	31.		Fourth Army Aux. H.T. Coy. left Divl. area for ALBERT.	
			*****	
			The weather during the month has been generally fine.	

J.A.S. Lieut Major Arc
A.D.V.S. 19 Division

59

1875 Wt. W593/826 1,000,000 4/15 I.R.C. & A. A.D.S.S./Forms/C. 2118.

Instructions regarding War Diaries and Intelligence Summaries are contained in F. S. Regs., Part II. and the Staff Manual respectively. Title Pages will be prepared in manuscript.

WAR DIARY
~~or~~
~~INTELLIGENCE~~ SUMMARY
(Erase heading not required.)

Army Form C. 2118

ADVS 18 Div
Vol 10

Place	Date 1916	Hour	Summary of Events and Information	Remarks and references to Appendices
ETINEHEM	May 1		ADVS on leave to England. Capt E.E. Gellant to officiate 15 sick horses evacuated to Base.	
..	.. 5		D.H.Q. moved to CAVILLON into rest area. 82 + 85 Bdes RFA remaining with 30 Div also field Coys R.E. M.T. Sect D.A.C. and 54 Inf Bde. Capt Williams and Lt O'Connor remain with their Bdes + also take charge of other units of 18 Div left in 30 Div area. Furnished ADVS 30 Div with list of units remaining and VOs &c and asked him to arrange Vety attendance for 150 Coy 18 Div Train at SAILLY LAURETTE. Disposition of VOs in new area. Capt Gellant 30 MVS + 54 Fd Amb PICQUIGNY. also acting ADVS. Capt Austin { 83 Bde RFA at ARGOEUVRE. 53 Inf Bde at AILLY SUR SOMME, LONGPRE VAUX + ST SAUVEUR 55 Fd Amb BERTANGLES Capt Thompson 84 Bde RFA at ST SAUVEUR. 55 Inf Bde PICQUIGNY, ST PIERRE à Gouy Lt Bradley DHQ Signal Coy CAVILLON. 3 Coys 18 Div Train AILLY-SUR-SOMME HQ 54 Bde + 54 MG Coy OISSY 56 Fd Amb SAISSEMONT Div Cav Sqn BREILLY	
CAVILLON	.. 7		Redistribution of smoke helmets. horses made some being withdrawn from Inf Bdes back in rest + re issued to RA units remaining up + doing fatigue work too from the trenches.	60

1875 Wt. W593/826 1,000,000 4/15 J.B.C. & A. A.D.S.S./Forms/C. 2118.

Instructions regarding War Diaries and Intelligence Summaries are contained in F. S. Regs., Part II. and the Staff Manual respectively. Title Pages will be prepared in manuscript.

Army Form C. 2118

WAR DIARY
or
INTELLIGENCE SUMMARY
(Erase heading not required.)

Place	Date 1916	Hour	Summary of Events and Information	Remarks and references to Appendices
CAVILLON	May 11		ADVS returned from leave & took over Vety charge of DHQ & 18 Signal Coy RE.	
..	.. 13		Visited RA at St SAUVEUR – weather good & horses should improve. B/84 looking worst in condition.	
..	.. 14		Capt SR Gilbert on leave to England. Major Verney i/c No 30 Mob Vet Sec	
..	.. 16		8 sick horses evacuated to Base.	
..	.. 18		Inspected 153 Coy ASC & found about a dozen thin horses transferred from 150 Coy, advised resting these as much as possible as clearly suffering from overwork. Northumberland Hussars (XIII Corps Cavalry) arrived into 18 Div area and Lt Bradley put in Vety charge. Located at BRIQUEMESNIL.	
	19	..	Visited N. Hussars. Sent case of suspected Sarcoptic mange to M.V.S. – another suspicious case isolated for further observation. Horses generally in very fair condition although some rather thin.	
			Found Sarcopt in scraping from horse of N Hussars sent to MVS.	
..	.. 20		Reorganisation of RA DAC taking place – BACs absorbed into DAC which will have 4 sections and Howitzer Bde divided amongst other Bdes. D Btys of each Bde being taken to form 85 Bde of field batteries.	61

1875 Wt. W593/826 1,000,000 4/15 J.B.C. & A. A.D.S.S./Forms/C. 2118.

Army Form C. 2118

Instructions regarding War Diaries and Intelligence Summaries are contained in F. S. Regs., Part II. and the Staff Manual respectively. Title Pages will be prepared in manuscript.

WAR DIARY
or
~~INTELLIGENCE SUMMARY~~
(Erase heading not required.)

Place	Date 1916	Hour	Summary of Events and Information	Remarks and references to Appendices
CAVILLON	May 22		Visited Details RA with DAQMG to pick out remounts for DHQ units before they leave for the Base. Found a number of heavy horses amongst them which RA Bdes had changed without referring to the VO i/c although these horses are going to Base for re issue to other units. Sent 5 to MVS & instructed Capt Austin to carefully examine all the horses & mules tomorrow & send any unfit into MVS	
			53 Inf Bde marched out to join 30 Div	
			Indented for 250 more Smoke helmets horses in order to give a small number to all units likely to be exposed to Gas.	
"	" 23		Inspected horses present at MVS. 14 evacuated to Base	
			Visited Details RA & found Capt Austin had picked out 18 for MVS.	
"	" 25		Capt Gellatt returned from leave	
"	" 26		Found Sarcopt in scraping from Brady B Squad N Hussars	
			16 Sick horses evacuated to Base	
"	" 27		Inspected N. Hussars and sent 2 Horses to MVS.	
"	" 29		Capt Thompson returned to England, Capt Austin taking charge of his RA & Capt Gellatt 53 Inf Bde.	62

1875 Wt. W593/826 1,000,000 4/15 J.B.C. & A. A.D.S.S./Forms/C. 2118.

Army Form C. 2118

Instructions regarding War Diaries and Intelligence Summaries are contained in F. S. Regs., Part II. and the Staff Manual respectively. Title Pages will be prepared in manuscript.

WAR DIARY
or
~~INTELLIGENCE SUMMARY~~

(Erase heading not required.)

Place	Date 1916	Hour	Summary of Events and Information	Remarks and references to Appendices
CAVILLON	May 30		Wrote letter to DDVS suggesting that if an order, making clipping compulsory in September and October for all horses, could be issued, the disability next winter both from skin disease and debility might be considerably lessened & that if orders were issued again horses could be kept regularly clipped during the winter.	

[illegible] Major
ADVS. 18 Division

63

1875 Wt. W593/826 1,000,000 4/15 J.B.C. & A. A.D.S.S./Forms/C. 2118.

Instructions regarding War Diaries and Intelligence Summaries are contained in F. S. Regs., Part II. and the Staff Manual respectively. Title Pages will be prepared in manuscript.

WAR DIARY ~~or~~ INTELLIGENCE SUMMARY

(Erase heading not required.)

Army Form C. 2118

ADVS 18 D

Vol 11

Place	Date 1916	Hour	Summary of Events and Information	Remarks and references to Appendices
CAVILLON	June 8.		Capt Williams ~~returned from~~ leave to England.	
	9		Capt Thompson returned from leave.	
	10		RA left ARGOEUVRES for Bois de Tailles. Capt Thompson sick to hospital with German measles.	
			Capt Austin accompanied RA of 83 & 84 Bdes to 30 Div area.	
	13		Visited Railhead 5.30 A.M. and issued 60 Remounts for 18 Div.	
			10 Sick evacuated by 30 MVS.	
	14		Inspected 54 Inf Bde transport back from forward area to PICQUIGNY. All looking well especially Bedford Regt.	
			Recd from ADV Stores 6 cases instruments for Officers wallets and farriers wallets for D.H.Q.	
			Sent DDVS my scheme for Vety arrangements in event of an offensive which I had previously arranged with A & Q.	
			Advanced Collecting Post at BOIS DE TAILLES and rest of section at SAILLY-LE-SEC	
	17		Visited Bois de Tailles with O.C. MVS to pick site for ADV Collecting Post.	64
	18		Attended conference at office of DDVS Fourth Army.	

1875 Wt. W593/826 1,000,000 4/15 J.B.C. & A. A.D.S.S./Forms/C. 2118.

Army Form C. 2118

Instructions regarding War Diaries and Intelligence Summaries are contained in F. S. Regs., Part II. and the Staff Manual respectively. Title Pages will be prepared in manuscript.

WAR DIARY
~~or~~
INTELLIGENCE ~~SUMMARY~~

(Erase heading not required.)

Place	Date 1916	Hour	Summary of Events and Information	Remarks and references to Appendices
CAVILLON	June 23		D.H.Q moved to ETINEHEM. GOC to Battle H.Q and A & Q in [illegible]. 30 MVS to SAILLY LE SEC. Capt Thompson rejoined for duty from hospital	
ETINEHEM	" 24		An advanced case of sarcoptic mange sent in from A/82 which V.O. only considered to be a bit suspicious. This horse came as a remount about 3 months ago and must have been affected then. I cannot help thinking that the majority of cases of sarcoptic mange are in horses which have not been thoroughly cured before re-issue – recently this has certainly been the case.	
"	" 25		A.D.V. Collecting Post established at Bois de Tailles + sign posts put up at various places showing the way to it.	
	" 26		Visited Bois de Tailles + inspected A/82, picked out another case of sarcoptic mange (also a recent arrival) + one suspected, to go to M.V.S. Showed all V.O.s where Collecting Post situated + instructed them to give their cases first aid there if necessary. Capt Thompson sick to hospital again. Telegraphed to D.D.V.S for relief.	65
	27		17 Sick evacuated by M.V.S including 2 of 30 Div.	

1875 Wt. W593/826 1,000,000 4/15 J.B.C. & A. A.D.S.S./Forms/C. 2118.

Instructions regarding War Diaries and Intelligence Summaries are contained in F. S. Regs., Part II. and the Staff Manual respectively. Title Pages will be prepared in manuscript.

WAR DIARY

or

~~INTELLIGENCE SUMMARY~~

(Erase heading not required.)

Army Form C. 2118

Place	Date	Hour	Summary of Events and Information	Remarks and references to Appendices
	1916			
ETINEHEM	June 28		Disposition of V.O's & units during offensive operations.	
			Capt Gilbert 30 M.V.S. SAILLY LE SEC – Adv Collecting Post BOIS DE TAILLES	
			Capt Austin, BOIS DE TAILLES 83 Bde RFA Bois de Tailles & 54 Inf Bde & Sussex Pioneers GROVETOWN	
			" (Temp) " 84 Bde " " 55 " "	
			Capt Williams " 82 Bde " " 53 " "	
			Lt O'Connor 85 Bde " " 79, 80 & 92 Field Coys RE "	
			Lt Bradley CHIPILLY 18 Div Train CHIPILLY, DAC SAILLY LAURETTE & SAILLY LE SEC	
			53 Field Amb "	
			Visited Railhead and issued 56 Remounts for the Division.	
			M.V.S. will evacuate horses at MERICOURT, where an extra 20 men AVC are stationed to go down with the trucks instead of men from M.V. Sections. This is an excellent arrangement & saves depleting the sections of men at a time when all available may be urgently required.	
			[signature] Major	
			ADVS 18 Div	66

1875 Wt. W593/826 1,000,000 4/15 J.B.C. & A. A.D.S.S./Forms/C. 2118.

67

18 Vol 12
ADVS

A.D.V.S.
18TH DIVISION.

Instructions regarding War Diaries and Intelligence Summaries are contained in F. S. Regs., Part II. and the Staff Manual respectively. Title pages will be prepared in manuscript.

WAR DIARY
or
INTELLIGENCE SUMMARY.
(Erase heading not required.)

Army Form C. 2118.

Place	Date	Hour	Summary of Events and Information	Remarks and references to Appendices
	1916			68
ETINEHEM	July 1		British attack commenced 7.30 A.M.	
			Lieut W.R. CAMERON reported for duty vice Capt Thompson evacuated sick – posted 84 Bde RFA	
			Met all V.Os at ADV Collecting Post of 30 MVS at BOIS DETAILLES and explained to them the arrangements for evacuation of sick and wounded animals.	
			The M.V.S will clear the ADV Post every evening to the Section at SAILLY LE SEC and evacuate from railhead almost daily when possible to get trucks in order to avoid congestion.	
NE of BRAY	" 4		Q Branch 18th Div HQ moved up to dug outs NE of BRAY where G has been since commencement of operations.	
"	" 5		My clerk Pte McLeod evacuated sick with Asthma. Wired DDVS for a relief	
"	" 7		S/3 No 023954 Pte E.J. HAYNES ASC from 18 DSC arrived for duty as clerk to ADVS. Met all V.Os and gave each a new Field Case Bk also copies of DVS Circ memo re Penetrable injuries.	
"	" 8		DHQ moved back to GROVETOWN on relief by 3rd Div.	
			So far casualties in animals from gunfire very slight most of evacuations being for debility and exhaustion owing to the very hard work ~~[illegible]~~ endured by the RA horses in carting ammunition. RA still in action.	

T.134. Wt. W708–776. 500000. 4/15. Sir J. C. & S.

Army Form C. 2118.

Instructions regarding War Diaries and Intelligence Summaries are contained in F. S. Regs., Part II. and the Staff Manual respectively. Title pages will be prepared in manuscript.

WAR DIARY
or
INTELLIGENCE SUMMARY.
(Erase heading not required.)

Place	Date	Hour	Summary of Events and Information	Remarks and references to Appendices
	1916			
GROVETOWN CAMP	July 10		85 Bde RFA moved back to BOIS DETAILLES and A Echelon up to BOIS de Tailles.	
			B echelon from SAILLY LE SEC to SAILLY LAURETTE.	
			Lt Vicanner put in charge of A Echelon and Field Coys RE divided amongst other VOs	
			Several cases of mange & suspected mange occurring, chiefly traced to recently joined Remounts.	
"	" 16		Visited Railhead (HEILLY) ~~for~~ to view Remounts.	
			85 Bde moved up into the line for action.	
"	" 17		38 horses killed in action by shell fire and 34 wounded. 85 Bde RFA and 18 Signal Coy RE being chief sufferers	
"	" 18		As most of the Wagon lines RA have moved up am considering the advisability of moving my advanced Post of MVS nearer to them but as we are likely to move right back in a few days time do hardly think it worth while. Up to the present the original scheme has worked very well and it is more convenient for the section to be located as near as possible to Railhead as they can then find out if trucks are available before taking horses to the Station. ~~Hav~~ It has been possible to evacuate from MERICOURT instead of HEILLY and thus get the benefit of the special men	69

T. 131. Wt. W708–776. 500000. 4/15. Sir J. C. & S.

Instructions regarding War Diaries and Intelligence Summaries are contained in F. S. Regs., Part II. and the Staff Manual respectively. Title pages will be prepared in manuscript.

WAR DIARY
or
~~INTELLIGENCE SUMMARY.~~

(Erase heading not required.)

Army Form C. 2118.

Place	Date 1916	Hour	Summary of Events and Information	Remarks and references to Appendices
GROVETOWN	July 18		attached there for going down with the horses.	
..	.. 20		Infantry, RE, Div Train and Fd Ambulances left for HALLENCOURT area by road (2 marches) also MVS as all RA Vety Officers will be left behind till RA. move and there will only be the Train V.O. with this part of the Div.	
			RA to be attached to 35 Div until brought out. Called to see ADVS 35 Div & finding him out left note giving names & attachments of my V.Os with Art Bdes.	
..	21		DHQ left GROVETOWN for HALLENCOURT.	
HALLENCOURT	.. 22		MVS arrived LONGPRE in evening.	
			82 Bde RFA arrived ALLERY in evening.	
..	.. 23		MVS evacuated a batch of sick (12) by road to No 22 V.H. ABBEVILLE as entraining [illegible].	
			Visited 82 Bde and advised V.O i/c to send any sick by road to ABBEVILLE, if necessary before he moves.	
	24		DHQ entrained PONT REMY for St OMER & marched to RENESCURE.	
			MVS to LYNDE.	
			Now in 2nd Army area.	70

T.134. Wt. W708–776. 500000. 4/15. Sir J. C. & S.

WAR DIARY
or
~~INTELLIGENCE~~ SUMMARY.
(Erase heading not required.)

Place	Date 1916	Hour	Summary of Events and Information	Remarks and references to Appendices
RENESCURE	July 25		Visited DDVS 2nd Army, HAZEBROUCK to report – not in.	
"	" 26		Visited DDVS and had an interview.	
			Saw Inf Bde AVC sergts who report infantry transport had arrived in good order. Sent Lt Bradley to visit RE field Coys at ~~Stap~~ STAPLE.	
"	" 28		RA arrived into EECKE area by rail to BAILLEUL.	
			Visited V.O.s and found 64 horses had been left in Fourth Army area evacuated to various Mobile Vet Sections before leaving GROVETOWN and sent in to No 22 VH ABBEVILLE en route to 2nd Army. The majority of these were injuries but also included 10 debility and 10 suspected mange cases	
	" 29		No 30 MVS moved to FLETRE	
			Inspected Otago Squadron 2nd Anzac Cav Regt injected with Mallein (intra dermo palpebral) by Capt Pellant on 27th. No reactions.	
"	" 30		Inspected 84 Bde horses and D/83 at EECKE. Many debilitated horses for evacn. which is only to be expected after the very hard work they had been doing during the operations on the SOMME. D/84 especially bad.	71
	" 31		Inspected 82 Bde horses. Although looking light, none debilitated enough to evacuate.	

Instructions regarding War Diaries and Intelligence Summaries are contained in F. S. Regs., Part II. and the Staff Manual respectively. Title pages will be prepared in manuscript.

WAR DIARY
or
~~INTELLIGENCE~~ SUMMARY.
(Erase heading not required.)

Army Form C. 2118.

Place	Date 1916	Hour	Summary of Events and Information	Remarks and references to Appendices
RENESCURE	July 31		Put [illegible] in D.R.O. headed Prevention of Mange advising working segregation whenever possible of all Remounts for one month & constant inspection by V.O. y/c also warning all concerned of the danger of old used standings & picketing posts and necessity for thorough disinfection under supervision of Vety officer.	
			Recent operations on the Somme from July 1st to 21st.	
			Arrangements for evacuation of sick & wounded animals worked smoothly & well & there was no difficulty in finding the ADV Collecting Post owing to the plentiful use of sign boards. By evacuating small numbers daily the O.C. MVS never got his lines congested and nearly always managed to get truck accomodation at MERICOURT. No difficulty was experienced in getting the horses along the roads as it was possible to use side roads nearly all the way.	
			Altogether about 200 cases were evacuated – ~~nearly half~~ about a third of these being gunshot wounds. About 50 animals died or had to be destroyed as a result of shrapnel wounds the greater proportion being R.A. animals. Most of the casualties occurred in action and wagon lines were comparatively free from shellfire until just at the end.	72

T.134. Wt. W708–776. 500000. 4/15. Sir J. C. & S.

Instructions regarding War Diaries and Intelligence Summaries are contained in F. S. Regs., Part II. and the Staff Manual respectively. Title pages will be prepared in manuscript.

WAR DIARY
or
INTELLIGENCE SUMMARY.
(*Erase heading not required.*)

Army Form C. 2118.

Place	Date 1916	Hour	Summary of Events and Information	Remarks and references to Appendices
RENESCURE	July 31.		The special men of the AVC posted at Railhead to go down with the trucks were always in great request and this arrangement was much appreciated by O.C. M.V.S., who had plenty of use for all his men between his Adv Post & Section. The presence of No 12 M.V.S. at Railhead to which these extra men were attached was also at times a great convenience as the O.C. was always most obliging & ready to help. The R.A. horses suffered greatly in loss of condition from the constant overwork they got during operations but apparently this is a military necessity attendant on such times and, as is natural, the batteries which had the fittest horses at the start did not get the same number of debility cases as those which had horses on the thin side before the heavy work commenced.	73

[signature] Major
A.D.V.S. 18 Div

T.131. Wt. W708–776. 500000. 4/15. Sir J. C. & S.

74

A.D.V.S.

18th Division

Vol 13

Instructions regarding War Diaries and Intelligence Summaries are contained in F. S. Regs., Part II. and the Staff Manual respectively. Title pages will be prepared in manuscript.

WAR DIARY
~~or~~
~~INTELLIGENCE SUMMARY.~~
(Erase heading not required.)

Army Form C. 2118.

Place	Date 1916	Hour	Summary of Events and Information	Remarks and references to Appendices
Le CROIX DU BAC	Aug 2		D.H.Q. marched from RENESCURE to CROIX DU BAC. areas RA wagon lines, Inf Transport and Fd Coys RE in the neighbourhood of ERQUINGHEM. DAC LE KIRLEM. Div Train CROIX DU BAC. M.V.S LE SEQUEMEAU. No change necessary in disposition of V.O's.	
	" 4		Visited BAILLEUL Station 9 am & issued 58 Remounts for DAQMG.	
	" 5		Took over administration of Sick Horse Barge service from ADVS 5 Aust Div.	
			Barge runs from BAC ST MAUR bridge to ST OMER every Tuesday & Friday leaving at 8 A.M. & is used by 5 Aust Div, NZ Div, 41 Div, 36 Div and 18 Div for cases unable to march to ST OMER. Foraging and embarkation supervised by OC MVS of Div administering it and each Div in turn to supply conducting party of 1 NCO and 2 men.	
			Marching cases proceed by road each Div having one day a week & using Sick horse halts on the way. One man to six horses tied together in pairs.	
			Barge service good for bad cases as no shunting & getting about but having only one day a week for emptying station rather apt to cause stagnation and	75

T.134. Wt. W708–776. 500000. 4/15. Sir J. C. & S.

Instructions regarding War Diaries and Intelligence Summaries are contained in F. S. Regs., Part II. and the Staff Manual respectively. Title pages will be prepared in manuscript.

WAR DIARY

~~or~~

~~INTELLIGENCE~~ SUMMARY.

(*Erase heading not required.*)

Army Form C. 2118.

Place	Date 1916	Hour	Summary of Events and Information	Remarks and references to Appendices
CROIX DU BAC	Aug. 5		to make mange cases look worse than when admitted by the time they reach hospital. No mange cases allowed in Barge.	
"	6		Visited No. 1 Sec DAC and sent 3 suspected mange cases to M.V.S.	
"	7		Sergt Sketchley AVC B/84 & Sergt Baker AVC No 3 Sec DAC reduced by C.M. for drunkenness to rank of Corporal	
"	9		Inspected 82 Bde RFA condition of horses improved especially B/82. Picked out a mange case in A/82 for M.V.S. and several suspected for isolation & daily dressing. V.O. appears unable to recognise mange in early stages and find this a failing in all V.O.s in spite of my endeavours to teach them.	
"	10		Inspected 83 Bde RFA – condition of horses improving.	
"	12		Attended conference of ADVS at BAILLEUL with DDVS 2nd Army. Subjects discussed – Increase in mange and measures to be adopted for prevention of same. Effects of Gas poisoning & respirators. Liability of presence of Glanders.	
"	13		Bad case of sarcoptic mange in A/83 and six cases of suspected mange in A/82 sent to M.V.S.	
"	14		Inspected 84 Bde RFA. Horses in A B & C batteries improving. D bad – many thin.	76

T.134. Wt. W708–776. 500000. 4/15. Sir J. C. & S.

Instructions regarding War Diaries and Intelligence Summaries are contained in F. S. Regs., Part II. and the Staff Manual respectively. Title pages will be prepared in manuscript.

WAR DIARY
~~or~~
~~INTELLIGENCE~~ SUMMARY.
(Erase heading not required.)

Army Form C. 2118.

Place	Date 1916	Hour	Summary of Events and Information	Remarks and references to Appendices
CROIX DU BAC	Aug 15		Inspected ASC. Horses looking in excellent condition. 1 suspected case of mange 150 Coy to MVS & 1 bad case sarcoptic 151 Coy. This horse has been isolated but not diagnosed by VO although a typical case of some standing – other horses fit & clean.	
"	" 19		Sent 4 suspected cases of mange from A/82 to MVS and 6 from No 4 Sec DAC. These six were all remounts received from ABBEVILLE less than a month ago and a [illegible] was found by OC MVS on one of them today.	
"	" 20		Sketchley & Baker left for No 2 VH. to be relieved by A/Sergt Sanders and Humphreys.	
"	" 22		Sent 2 more Remounts from No 4 DAC to MVS for suspected mange. DDVS visited 83 and 84 Bdes RFA and MVS. He considered RA horses good except D/84 and advised my to be [illegible] for Debility from this battery. Reported cases of mange from No 4 Sec DAC & showed him the two horses sent in in the morning.	
	" 23		Visited STEENWERCK station and issued 142 Remounts for DAQMG. Lt Cameron accompanied me and examined all these animals for suspected skin diseases before they left the station.	
	" 24		Handed over Barge service to ADVS 34 Div. DHQ moved to BAILLEUL.	
	22		Wrote to AA & QMG advising all horses should be clipped in September & regularly after to keep down lice & mange.	77

T.2134. Wt. W708–776. 500000. 4/15. Sir J. C. & S.

Instructions regarding War Diaries and Intelligence Summaries are contained in F. S. Regs., Part II. and the Staff Manual respectively. Title pages will be prepared in manuscript.

WAR DIARY
or
~~INTELLIGENCE SUMMARY.~~

(Erase heading not required.)

Army Form C. 2118.

Place	Date 1916	Hour	Summary of Events and Information	Remarks and references to Appendices
BAILLEUL	Aug 26		DHQ entrained 10. A.M. and detrained St POL 2 PM - marched to ROELLECOURT Inf, RE ASC (less 1 Coy) in this area. RA to arrive later. MVS to LE QUESNEL	
ROELLECOURT	" 27		Visited DDVS Third Army at St POL	
	" 28		Lt Bradley (18 Div Train VO) sick - other VOs with RA Bdes not yet arrived.	
			ADVS i/c DHQ, 18 Signal Coy ROELLECOURT 56 FA L'ABBAYE de NEUVILLE farm	
			53 Inf Bde CHELERS and surrounding area 79 Fd Coy RE BETHENCOURT	
			54 Inf Bde LA THIEULOYE and area. 80 Fd Coy RE & 54 Fd Amb.	
			53 Inf Bde MONCHY BRETON .. .. 92 RE. MAGNICOURT & 55 F.A. TINCQUETTE	
			152 Coy ASC MARQUAY	
	"		Capt Gilbert i/c MVS LE QUESNEL 151 & 153 ASC TINQUES 8 R Sussex Pioneers AVERDOINGT	
	" 30		Told by A that R.A. will not come to this area but proceed straight to forward area & be attached to 4 Aust Div. Sent DRLS to Capt Austin VO 83 Bde telling him to send his A2000 to ADVS 4 Aust Div and inform other R.A. VOs to do likewise.	
	" 31		Lieut Bradley evacuated to No. 12 Hospital.	

[illegible] Major
ADVS. 18. Div

78

T2134. Wt. W708-776. 500000. 4/15. Sir J. C. & S.

Instructions regarding War Diaries and Intelligence Summaries are contained in F. S. Regs., Part II. and the Staff Manual respectively. Title pages will be prepared in manuscript. ADVS 18th Div

WAR DIARY ~~or~~ ~~INTELLIGENCE SUMMARY.~~

(Erase heading not required.)

Army Form C. 2118.

VOL 14

Place	Date 1916	Hour	Summary of Events and Information	Remarks and references to Appendices
ROELLCOURT	Sept 1.		Lt J Bradley AVC evacuated to Base for Sciatica.	
..	.. 2		Wired DDVS 3rd Army for relief for Lt Bradley..	
..	.. 3		Received R.A. A2000 from VOs by post after my return headquarters in so considered them & forwarded on to DDVS Reserve Army to which RA are attached & 150 to ASC.	
..	.. 5		Move of Div cancelled for the present.	
..	.. 6		Lieut W.F. MACDOUGALL arrived for duty ~~[illegible]~~ vice Lt Bradley & posted to 18 Div Train also took over charge of Infantry Brigades RE & Fd Ambulances from me.	
..	.. 8		Visited Railhead to view 26 Remounts for DAQMG.	
DOULLENS	.. 9		DHQ marched to DOULLENS.	
ACHEUX.	.. 11		.. .. .. ACHEUX.	
..	.. 12		Visited DDVS Reserve Army.	
			Disposition of VOs. Major VERNEY i/c DHQ & 18 Signal Coy RE ACHEUX.	
			Capt JELBART (ACHEUX) i/c 30 MVS also 53 Inf Bde & 56 FA & 79 RE LEALVILLERS & ACHEUX	
			Capt MACDOUGALL (ACHEUX) i/c 18 Div Train also 54 Inf Bde, 55 Inf Bde, 80 & 92 RE, 54 & 55 FA. at LEALVILLERS - RAINCHEVAL, ARQUEVES & PUCHEVILLERS.	79
..	.. 13		Sergt SOUTHALL AVC att 55 Inf Bde sick to Fd Amb.	

T.134. Wt. W708-776. 500000. 4/15. Sir J. C. & S.

Instructions regarding War Diaries and Intelligence Summaries are contained in F. S. Regs., Part II. and the Staff Manual respectively. Title pages will be prepared in manuscript.

ADVS 18th Div

WAR DIARY
~~or~~
~~INTELLIGENCE SUMMARY.~~
(Erase heading not required.)

Army Form C. 2118.

Place	Date 1916	Hour	Summary of Events and Information	Remarks and references to Appendices
ACHEUX	Sept 14		Visited 150 Bde Train at SENLIS. Several thin horses & all fallen off in condition owing to hard work.	
"	" 16		Visited RA wagon lines att to 2 Can Div & saw my V.Os.	
			Received RA A2000 sent me by ADVS 2 Can Div after my A2000 had gone in, sent them back & asked him to include them in his as RA att to his Div for administration.	
"	" 18		RA A2000 sent back to me by ADVS 2 Can Div who disclaimed any knowledge of 18 Div RA being under his administration, so sent them in direct to DDVS late & will administer them myself for the future. Lieut O'Connor sick to field ambulance.	
"	" 19		Visited Railhead and inspected 70 Remounts for DAQMG.	
"			Visited Col Cameron 84 Bde RFA re confidential letter from IGC.	
"	" 20		Visited 84 Bde RFA near ALBERT. All thin & fallen off in condition especially D/84 which is very bad indeed. Picked out 25 horses which urgently require to be evacuated & should have gone long before.	
			Informed by 53 Bde that Sergt SOUTHALL evacuated to base on 15th. Applied to DDVS for relief.	
"	21		Saw DAQMG with reference to sending an urgent indent for 25 horses to replace the 25 I propose to evacuate from D/84 & wrote CRA informing him of this.	80
			8 of these horses sent into MVS today all in deplorable condition.	

T.134. Wt. W708-776. 500000. 4/15. Sir J. C. & S.

Instructions regarding War Diaries and Intelligence Summaries are contained in F. S. Regs., Part II. and the Staff Manual respectively. Title pages will be prepared in manuscript. ADVS 18th Div

WAR DIARY

~~or~~

~~INTELLIGENCE SUMMARY.~~

(Erase heading not required.)

Army Form C. 2118.

Place	Date 1916	Hour	Summary of Events and Information	Remarks and references to Appendices
ACHEUX	Sept 22		Visited 150 Coy ASC & picked out 4 horses for early evacuation for debility.	
	" 23		Visited RA wagon lines and impressed on V.Os the necessity for preventing horses in their charge from getting very badly debilitated by constant attention & evacuation when necessary so that they will never have a large number going away at one time as is the case in D/84. Civilian V.Os are rather inclined to wait until their attention is directed to sick animals instead of picking them out for themselves, which is very necessary in new army units where many of the officers of wagon lines don't seem to know when a horse is going all to pieces or don't care so long as they can manage to get one leg in front of the other. The work of the RA horses is very severe & always will be when an offensive is in progress consequently there is bound to be a much higher percentage of wastage than in ordinary times & the only way to prevent this from being felt by the units is to keep evacuating small numbers as they occur so that the first batch will have been replaced by the time the second is due to go & in such a condition that they can be received & re-issued in a few months.	
"	" 24		All day at Railhead waiting to issue Remounts for D/84 specially wired for by DAQMG. 24 arrived.	81
"	" 25		DHQ moved to HEDAUVILLE also MVS, HQ Div Train & Inf Bdes.	

WAR DIARY
or
~~INTELLIGENCE~~ SUMMARY.
(Erase heading not required.)

Army Form C. 2118.

Instructions regarding War Diaries and Intelligence Summaries are contained in F. S. Regs., Part II. and the Staff Manual respectively. Title pages will be prepared in manuscript.

ADVS 18th Div

Place	Date 1916	Hour	Summary of Events and Information	Remarks and references to Appendices
HEDAUVILLE	Sept 26		THIEPVAL attacked & taken by 18 Div Infantry.	
			Took over administration of 49 Div Artillery, 41 Bde 2nd Div and 1/1 WR MVS 49 Div all attached to 18 Div.	
			The other 19 debility cases sent in from A/84 to MVS, all in shocking condition.	
"	" 27		Visited RA wagon lines and marked down 9 debility cases from A/84 for evacuation.	
"	" 28		Visited Railhead (ACHEUX) & issued 94 Remounts from DAQMG (61 for RA)	
			Visited A/84 VO informs me that OC of Bty has given orders that the 9 debility cases are not to be sent away till other horses have arrived. The VO of this Bde has frequently been interfered with in the evacuation of horses which are not fit to stay so will write to CRA as this cannot be allowed if the Vety service is to be efficient.	
"	" 29		Wrote to CRA & enclosed letter written to me by OC 84 Bde & one from OC A/84 to O i/c Wagon lines re evacuating these 9 horses. Pointed out that they were quite unfit for work & only putting extra strain on the other horses & that I should consider their condition to be a serious reflection on the VO i/c if I did not feel convinced that he had been hindered in performing his duty in the matter. Description & numbers of these horses also stated.	82

T.134. Wt. W708–776. 500000. 4/15. Sir J. C. & S.

Instructions regarding War Diaries and Intelligence Summaries are contained in F. S. Regs., Part II. and the Staff Manual respectively. Title pages will be prepared in manuscript.

WAR DIARY
~~or~~
~~INTELLIGENCE~~ SUMMARY.

(Erase heading not required.)

Army Form C. 2118.

Place	Date	Hour	Summary of Events and Information	Remarks and references to Appendices
	1916			
HEDAUVILLE	Apl 30		Over 100 cases of debility admitted in returns for the week mostly RA horses, representation made to AA&QMG pointing this out and that it was the result of overwork the following being contributing causes.	
			"Long distances from wagon lines to guns.	
			Bad roads to gun positions (particularly in wet weather)	
			Length of time spent in draught (frequently all night)	
			Irregularity of watering & feeding owing to urgency of demands."	
			This of course is military necessity & will always occur when a great offensive is in progress therefore more horses will be used up & the most economical thing to be done is to get them sent to the Base before their condition is hopeless.	
			It would be very advantageous if there was an advanced Remount depot where a certain number of horses could be kept for urgent demands, within walking distance of the units, as under the present system of indenting for Remounts the indents are sent in once a fortnight & horses do not arrive for a week after the indent has gone through this is a serious handicap to a unit losing a large no. at one time.	
			Wrote to DAQMG suggesting that when an offensive was in progress horse indents might be sent in twice a week if necessary.	83
			[illegible] Major ADVS. 18. Div	

Vol ~~14~~ 15

Army Form C. 2118.

Instructions regarding War Diaries and Intelligence Summaries are contained in F. S. Regs., Part II. and the Staff Manual respectively. Title pages will be prepared in manuscript.

WAR DIARY
~~or~~
~~INTELLIGENCE SUMMARY.~~

(Erase heading not required.)

Place	Date 1916	Hour	Summary of Events and Information	Remarks and references to Appendices
			ADVS. 18. Division Vol. 16.	
HEDAUVILLE	Oct. 2		Lieut S F COTTON AVC (TC), reported for duty vice Lt O'Connor evacuated sick & posted to 83 Bde RFA. Recommended Capt S E Pollard on AF W3121 for consistently efficient performance of his duties. Received Standing Orders for distribution to VO's & AVC Sergts – a copy for each detailing the duties of AVC Sergts their position as regards the VO & OC unit to which attached etc. In my opinion this supplies a long felt want & should prove very useful to all concerned.	
	" 3		Interviewed CRA & Staff Capt RA with reference to Debility cases & immediate evacuation of certain horses of 84 Bde forming the subject of a letter to CRA. Horses ordered to MVS. immediately. 49 Div RA & Mobile Vet Sec moved away to join 49. Div.	
	" 5		Interviewed ADVS 39 Div re attachment of 18 Div art to 39 Div temporarily.	
BERNAVILLE	" 6		Div HQ marched to BERNAVILLE with Infantry & Train (less 1 Coy). MVS to LE QUESNEL FARM. OC MVS i/c 53 Inf Bde & 56 FA. VO 18 Div Train i/c 54 & 55 Inf Bdes 54 & 55 FA & Pioneers RE all in BERNAVILLE area.	84
	9		Attended Conference at DDVS HQ Reserve Army.	

T.2134. Wt. W708-776. 500000. 4/15. Sir J. C. & S.

Instructions regarding War Diaries and Intelligence Summaries are contained in F. S. Regs., Part II. and the Staff Manual respectively. Title pages will be prepared in manuscript.

WAR DIARY or INTELLIGENCE SUMMARY.

(Erase heading not required.)

Army Form C. 2118.

Place	Date 1916	Hour	Summary of Events and Information	Remarks and references to Appendices
BERNAVILLE	Oct 11		ADVS on leave to England. Capt [illegible] officiating.	
ALBERT	.. 16		Division moved to ALBERT. 18th Div Art rejoined Division from attachment to 39th Div	
..	.. 21		ADVS returned to duty from leave. Nothing of importance has happened in his absence. Stewart Clipping Machines issued to units.	
..	.. 23		Wrote into AA&QMG expressing the opinion that horserugs are both unnecessary & wasteful for unclipped horses & recommending an R.O. prohibiting their use unless horses are clipped (except for sick animals). I know from previous experience that unless there is an order on the subject the use of rugs will be abused with the result that when they are really required most of them will be worn out.	
..	.. 25		Heavy rain lately & horse lines in a very bad state. Time & materials not available to build standings and many of the wagon lines not situated in suitable places. RA horses still working day & night & many debility cases occurring. Have impressed on VOs the necessity of sending them away before they reach the last stages.	85
..	.. 26		attended ACHEUX railhead 6.30 pm & issued 261 Remounts for DAQMG	
..	.. 29		sent DVS (through DDVS) a cheque for 394 francs subscribed by AVC. 18 Div. to Kitchener Memorial Fund.	

Instructions regarding War Diaries and Intelligence Summaries are contained in F. S. Regs., Part II. and the Staff Manual respectively. Title pages will be prepared in manuscript.

WAR DIARY
or
~~INTELLIGENCE SUMMARY.~~
(Erase heading not required.)

Army Form C. 2118.

Place	Date 1916	Hour	Summary of Events and Information	Remarks and references to Appendices
ALBERT	Oct 30		Wrote in to H.Q. R.A. re Debility cases pointing out the necessity for not trotting horses with returning empty wagons & raising the clipping trace high at least, to prevent sweating etc. Copies to AA&QMG 18 Div & DDVS ~~[illegible]~~ Reserve Army.	
"	" 31		Wrote in to AA&QMG re condition of watering places for horses in vicinity of ALBERT. CRA is circulating a copy of my letter of yesterday to all unit Commanders. The ignorance of people in charge of horses as to how they should be used in their work & their capacity for endurance often strikes me as extraordinary & is no doubt largely responsible for the pitiful condition many are soon reduced to whenever extra work has to be done.	
			[illegible] Major ADVS. 18 Div	

86

Instructions regarding War Diaries and Intelligence Summaries are contained in F. S. Regs., Part II. and the Staff Manual respectively. Title pages will be prepared in manuscript.

WAR DIARY
or
INTELLIGENCE SUMMARY.
(Erase heading not required.)

Army Form C. 2118.

ADVS 18 D

Vol 16

Place	Date 1916	Hour	Summary of Events and Information	Remarks and references to Appendices
			ADVS 18 Div Vol 19.	
ALBERT	Nov 2		Attended Railhead for DAQMG & waited all day for Remounts to issue 14 to 18 Div.	
..	.. 3		Inspected No 3 Sec D.A.C. Horses & mules in excellent condition and a credit to the O.C. The condition of this unit shews what can be done even under the existing hard circumstances. Interviewed all VOs in my office & requested them to send in more careful & accurate descriptions with sick horses transferred to M.V.S pointing out that this is a thing in which the vety sergeants should be able to give valuable assistance.	
..	.. 4		DDVS fifth army visited my office. Sergts Corfield & Marsh (AVC) arrived to do duty with D/83 & C/85 respectively.	
..	.. 10		Met C.R.A. when visiting 83 Bde and accompanied him round. Endeavoured to persuade him that clipping at least trace high is very beneficial. He agrees with me regarding the evacuation of debilitated horses before they get too bad. Staff Capt 55 Inf Bde reports that 16 pack animals were killed last night by gas shells on the advanced transport lines. Owing to a barrage between the men & the horse lines the former were unable to get to them to do anything so that even had they had suitable gas helmets they could not have been put on.	

87

T.2134. Wt. W708–776. 500000. 4/15. Sir J. C. & S.

Instructions regarding War Diaries and Intelligence Summaries are contained in F. S. Regs., Part II. and the Staff Manual respectively. Title pages will be prepared in manuscript.

WAR DIARY
~~or~~
~~INTELLIGENCE SUMMARY.~~
(Erase heading not required.)

Army Form C. 2118.

Place	Date 1916	Hour	Summary of Events and Information	Remarks and references to Appendices
ALBERT	Nov 11		ADVS called at No 30 MVS when I was there. Told me that there was great difficulty in meeting all the demands for Remounts & therefore it would perhaps be advisable not to send away more debility cases for the present unless very bad.	
	12		Sent in Confidential Report on all AVC sergts re efficiency & reliability.	
	13		Visited Railhead to issue 209 Remounts for DAQMG due 5 PM. Train arrived 11:30 PM.	
	14		Visited 55 Heavy Art Group at request of Capt Blanchard AVC to see & confirm several cases of Influenza. Forwarded drug indent for this officer.	
	15		Weather very bad & all horses standing sinking in mud over fetlock deep. MVS very busy evacuating on an average about 40 daily, including animals of other Divisions and formations. Gangrenous ulceration of heels & coronets increasing daily & likely to under these conditions.	
	20		ADVS 61 Div called re his MVS taking over from No 30. He will administer RA & RE when HQ & Infantry move back to rest area.	
	21		Interviewed all V.Os & put Capt Williams i/c 150 Coy ASC & Capt Austin 80 & 92 RE & S. Pions which are remaining in the line with RA.	88
	22		D HQ left ALBERT for rest area.	

T.134. Wt. W708-776. 500000. 4/15. Sir J. C. & S.

Instructions regarding War Diaries and Intelligence Summaries are contained in F. S. Regs., Part II. and the Staff Manual respectively. Title pages will be prepared in manuscript.

WAR DIARY

~~or~~

~~INTELLIGENCE~~ SUMMARY.

(*Erase heading not required.*)

Army Form C. 2118.

Place	Date 1916	Hour	Summary of Events and Information	Remarks and references to Appendices
BUIGNY	NOV 23		Arrived at BUIGNY with DHQ. MVS at L' HEURE.	
	" 27		Disposition of units & VOs in new area.	
			53 Inf Bde LE TITRE, FOREST L' ABBAYE, HAUTVILLERS & LAMOTTE BULEUX } i/c Capt Macdougall	
			151 Co ASC LE TITRE 56 FA OUVILLE }	
			55 Inf Bde CANCHY, MARCHVILLE & DOMVAST. 153 Co ASC & 55 FA. 152 ASC }	
			54 Inf Bde DRUCAT, MILLENCOURT, NEUFMOULIN & NEUILLY L'HOPITAL & 54 FA. } i/c Capt Gellard	
			DHQ & 18 Signal Coy RE BUIGNY i/c Major Kenney	
	" 29		Sergt LANDER AVC evacuated to ENGLAND sick (54 Inf Bde). Applied to DDVS for a relief.	
	30		Called at HQ 7 C to see D.V.S. (not in).	
	"		All infantry horses & ASC ones under cover in buildings.	

[signature] Major
ADVS. 18 Div

89

T.134. Wt. W708-776. 500000. 4/15. Sir J. C. & S.

Instructions regarding War Diaries and Intelligence Summaries are contained in F. S. Regs., Part II. and the Staff Manual respectively. Title pages will be prepared in manuscript.

WAR DIARY
or
INTELLIGENCE SUMMARY.
(Erase heading not required.)

ADVS 18 D

Army Form C. 2118.

Vol 17

Place	Date 1916	Hour	Summary of Events and Information	Remarks and references to Appendices
			ADVS 18 Div Vol. No. 18.	
BUIGNY-ST MACLOU	Dec 2		Capt E.E. Jelbart on leave to England. Capt Macdougall to take temporary charge of No 30. M.V.S	
	" 4		Called and had an interview with D.V.S. in his office.	
	" 6		RA & 150 Cmy ASC arrived into this area from the front.	
	" 7		Visited 83 Bde. Many thin horses. Two had to be destroyed for Exhaustion after the march down.	
	" 9		Visited 84 Bde & went round with O.C. Some thin horses in A & B. D Bty in very fair condition owing to their having had good stabling during the last six weeks. Horse lines in a very exposed position on the hill side. Endeavoured to impress on Bde & Battery Commanders the necessity for resting the horses as much as possible.	
	" 10		Orders received from Corps that MVS must evacuate mill at l'Heure as it is required for a scabies hospital. This is very unfortunate for MVS as they had just got comfortably settled with all their horses under cover & men in a good billet which they thoroughly deserve after the hard work & rough surroundings of the past six weeks.	

90

T.134. Wt. W708-776. 500000. 4/15. Sir J. C. & S.

Instructions regarding War Diaries and Intelligence Summaries are contained in F. S. Regs., Part II. and the Staff Manual respectively. Title pages will be prepared in manuscript.

WAR DIARY
~~or~~
INTELLIGENCE SUMMARY.

(*Erase heading not required.*)

Army Form C. 2118.

Place	Date 1916	Hour	Summary of Events and Information	Remarks and references to Appendices
BUIGNY-ST-MACLOU	Dec 11		Met DDVS at No 30 MVS & took him to see No 4 & 3 Sec DAC & 84 Bde. He called to see AA&QMG who was not in but saw DAA&QMG & expressed to him the hope that a good billet would be given the MVS & that every endeavour would be made to get standings made for the RA horses. At present they are all out in the open.	
"	" 13		Attended No 2 Remount Depot & took over & issued for DAQMG 4 [illegible] Remounts.	
			No 30 MVS moved from L'HEURE mill to LA HALLE farm	
"	" 14		Capt [illegible] returned from leave.	
"	" 15		Visited 150 Coy ASC & picked out 10 debility cases for evacuation. Horse lines bad in marshy ground which is very wet from constant rain & snow.	
"	" 16		Accompanied AA&QMG to MVS at LA HALLE farm & to look for another place for MVS as this is promised to 79 RE Coy. Showed him a number of debility cases from the RA sent in for evacuation.	
			Wrote in to AA&QMG with copy of A3000 saying that their horses are getting worse instead of improving due to the bad condition of standings & foul weather & recommending less fatigue work for No 4 Sec DAC & 150 ASC. Copy to DDVS for information. There is so much fatigue work to be done that the advantage of the rest area is often a farce.	91

T.134. Wt. W708-776. 500000. 4/15. Sir J. C. & S.

Instructions regarding War Diaries and Intelligence Summaries are contained in F. S. Regs., Part II. and the Staff Manual respectively. Title pages will be prepared in manuscript.

WAR DIARY

~~or~~

~~INTELLIGENCE SUMMARY.~~

(Erase heading not required.)

Army Form C. 2118.

Place	Date 1916	Hour	Summary of Events and Information	Remarks and references to Appendices
BUIGNY-St MACLOU	Dec. 18		Visited 82 Bde which has had a case of sarcoptic mange. This was only noticed when the animal had been clipped out & had been existing for at least 6 weeks if not more. Discovered another case of sarcoptic mange recent in the same Bty (A) during clipping the whole Bty.	
	19		1 case of psoroptic mange discovered in MVS in horse from D/82 sent in for debility. None of these mange cases have been detected for many months but I am not surprised at their recurrence & we shall never be without them until clipping is made compulsory in the autumn. It is impossible to discover them early when the horse has a long matted & dirty coat often plastered down with mud. Pte Haines my clerk on leave to England.	
	20		Went round 83 Bde with O.C. Horse lines in an appalling condition, in places mud to the hocks. It is impossible to expect many horses to improve under these circumstances & I have brought this to the notice of the AA&QMG. Apparently material cannot be obtained for standings to be erected & there is no other field available into which the horses can be moved. None of the thin horses in the RA have improved & it will be necessary to evacuate a large number to hospital for debility.	92

Army Form C. 2118.

Instructions regarding War Diaries and Intelligence Summaries are contained in F. S. Regs., Part II. and the Staff Manual respectively. Title pages will be prepared in manuscript.

WAR DIARY
or
INTELLIGENCE SUMMARY.
(Erase heading not required.)

Place	Date 1916	Hour	Summary of Events and Information	Remarks and references to Appendices
BUIGNY-ST MACLOU	Dec 21		No 30 MVS moved from LA HALLE farm to Buildings N of ABBEVILLE. Two Nissen Huts and a marquee had been erected for VO, office & men but standing accommodation for horses is rather limited. This may be increased when DAC moves out and the position is favourable [illegible] for units on VH.	
			Gave a lecture on horse management to young officers of RA.	
	23		93 cases examined this week for debility (from RA & 150th Coy ASC)	
	24		Wrote to Artillery re cases of mange which have recently occurred pointing out the difficulty of discovering such cases when horses have long coats & advising that A/82 Bty should be clipped as soon as possible & the necessity for officers & NCOs to use the utmost vigilance in assisting the VO to discover affected animals early.	
			Also wrote AA & QMG a report on mange cases & asked him to also urge that clipping be carried out as fast as possible. It is difficult to get this done when horses are standing out in continual wet weather.	
	26		Saw CRA & advised him that clipping is the only way to prevent a big outbreak of mange also that the general condition of the horses of the RA is not in my opinion good.	93

T2134. Wt. W708–776. 500000. 4/15. Sir J. C. & S.

Army Form C. 2118

Instructions regarding War Diaries and Intelligence Summaries are contained in F. S. Regs., Part II. and the Staff Manual respectively. Title Pages will be prepared in manuscript.

WAR DIARY
or
INTELLIGENCE SUMMARY

(Erase heading not required.)

Place	Date 1916	Hour	Summary of Events and Information	Remarks and references to Appendices
BUIGNY-ST MACLOU	Dec 29		Attended Conference at DDVS HQ Fifth Army. Arranged with ADVS 61 Div about taking over when the Div moves up to the line.	
	30		Took RA Officers to No 5 VH. where O.C. gave them a demonstration & showed them round the hospital.	

[illegible signature]
ADVS 18 Div

94

1875 Wt. W593/826 1,000,000 4/15 J.B.C. & A. A.D.S.S./Forms/C. 2118.

Army Form C. 2118

WAR DIARY
or
INTELLIGENCE SUMMARY

(Erase heading not required.)

Instructions regarding War Diaries and Intelligence Summaries are contained in F. S. Regs., Part II. and the Staff Manual respectively. Title Pages will be prepared in manuscript.

ADVS 18 D

Vol 18

Place	Date	Hour	Summary of Events and Information	Remarks and references to Appendices
	1917		ADVS. 18 Div Vol 19.	
BUIGNY-ST. MACLOU	Jan 2		18 Div Artʸ marched out to reinforce 61 Div Art in the line. Their horses have not benefited by the three weeks in the rest area owing to bad weather, want of shelters & standings, to which can be added the large amount of fatigue work which always has to be done when a division goes into a new area. They have been out exactly one month, eight days of which is taken up in marching to and from the rest area. I am afraid there is bound to be a large number of debility cases in the future if much work has to be done and the quality & condition of remounts received recently is much below the usual standard.	
			Gave all VOs a good stock of H.R. forms No. 1 so that any horses left on march shall be properly left & have intimated them to notify ADVS 61 Div immediately on arrival so as to waste no time in getting them collected.	
			Capt W.F. Macdougall on leave to England. Major Hamer i/c 54 & 55 Inf Bdes & 18 Div ASC &c Capt Gelland i/c 53 Bde Group.	
	" 5		Received report from OC No 5 V.H. that a horse of 18 DAC evacuated & destroyed in hospital was affected with ulcerative cellulitis.	
	" 6		Visited 152 Coy ASC & inspected horse with [illegible] mange – evacuated to MVS & clipping advised.	
	" 7		Visited No 14 V.H. & saw cases of ulcerative cellulitis which had been under treatment for about six weeks unsuccessfully & were going to be sold to the butcher.	95

Army Form C. 2118

- Instructions regarding War Diaries and Intelligence Summaries are contained in F. S. Regs., Part II. and the Staff Manual respectively. Title Pages will be prepared in manuscript.

WAR DIARY
or
INTELLIGENCE SUMMARY
(Erase heading not required.)

Place	Date 1917	Hour	Summary of Events and Information	Remarks and references to Appendices
BUIGNY-St MACLOU	Jan 10		Visited No 2 Remount Depot & issued to units 25 horses for D.A.Q.M.G.	
	" 11		No 30 M.V.S marched out with part of D.H.Q. for forward area. A.D.V.S & office remaining till 15th	
	" 15		Left BUIGNY 9 am & arrived HEDAUVILLE 4 PM, joined same evening by clerk & office	
			D.H.Q. at BOUZINCOURT [illegible] in relief of 61 Div (South Midland)	
HEDAUVILLE	" 16		M.V.S to MARTINSART taking over from M.V.S of 61 Div. and 31 sick horses left there.	
	" 17		Visited M.V.S & inspected sick horses sent in by various other units. 10 only fit to destroy	
			being in such a debilitated condition. Applied to D.H.Q. for a fatigue party to bury same –	
			supplied from nearest Inf Bde.	
	" 18		Inspected two horses left behind by 61 Div with 56 F.A. at Varennes. Both hopeless cases &	
			ordered their destruction. Snow & very severe cold.	
	" 19		Visited 82 Bde RFA & inspected 3 cases of Sarcoptic mange – evacuated to M.V.S	
			Sent in [illegible] for D.R.O. drawing attention to G.R.O 441 re Mange.	
			Disposition of units & V.Os.	
			Major Vlenning [illegible] 55 Inf Bde & 56 F.A at HEDAUVILLE and VARENNES & 55 F.A FORCEVILLE	
			Capt Gilbert No 30 MVS MARTINSART.	
			Capt Austin 83 Bde RFA in SENLIS & 53 & 54 Inf Bdes MARTINSART	
			~~Capt Wilkinson~~ 82 Bde RFA on right of Hedauville – Bouzincourt Rd & 84 Bde RFA	
			Lt Cameron 18 D.A.C Bouzincourt – Hedauville Rd & 150 Coy A.S.C Hedauville	
			Lt Cotton 18 Div Train less 1 Coy, D.H.Q, all R.E. & attached units	
			Capt Macdougall	
			Capt [illegible] [illegible] 61 Div Art att 18 Div for a few days	
				96

1875 Wt. W593/826 1,000,000 4/15 J.B.C. & A. A.D.S.S./Forms/C. 2118.

Instructions regarding War Diaries and Intelligence Summaries are contained in F. S. Regs., Part II. and the Staff Manual respectively. Title Pages will be prepared in manuscript.

WAR DIARY
or
INTELLIGENCE SUMMARY
(Erase heading not required.)

Army Form C. 2118

Place	Date 1917	Hour	Summary of Events and Information	Remarks and references to Appendices
HEDAUVILLE	Jan 20		No. 30 M.V.S. very congested with sick horses sent in by units of 61 Div & 11 Div before moving out. Evacuating daily so a lot of men down the line. Obtained outside assistance (for the first time) 5 RA & 3 ASC men. Numerous cases of horses absolutely exhausted, are dead on line during the night & many only fit to destroy.	
"	" 22		Inspected horses of 150 Coy ASC for contagious Stomatitis as 3 horses of this Coy recently sent down by S.M. MVS are reported to have been affected with this disease. No signs of any being affected in the Coy. Capt Williams returned from leave. 61 Div Art moved out.	
"	" 23		M.V.S. still flooded by horses from 61 & 11 Divisions. Obtained 12 Infantrymen for the day to assist in conducting them to railhead and 8 from RA for three days to send down the line.	
			Lt Cameron proceeded on leave.	
"	" 24		84 Bde RFA & No 3 Sec DAC now Fifth Army Troops but still attached to 18 Div.	
"	" 27		Visited ACHEUX railhead & issued 133 Remounts for DAC only – should have arrived yesterday but delayed by accident on line.	
"	28		Moved my office to BOUZINCOURT [illegible]. Weather extraordinary severe & cold N wind playing havoc with RA horses which are all out in the open especially affecting remounts received about [illegible] at Abbeville which were in rather poor condition & had most of them evidently come from mange hospital.	97

1875 Wt. W593/826 1,000,000 4/15 J.B.C. & A. A.D.S.S./Forms/C. 2118.

Army Form C. 2118

Instructions regarding War Diaries and Intelligence Summaries are contained in F. S. Regs., Part II. and the Staff Manual respectively. Title Pages will be prepared in manuscript.

WAR DIARY
or
INTELLIGENCE SUMMARY

(Erase heading not required.)

Place	Date	Hour	Summary of Events and Information	Remarks and references to Appendices
BOUZINCOURT	1917 Jan 28		The hot bath treatment for mange certainly does not ~~[illegible]~~ render horses fit & able to withstand exposure to severe cold weather & cutting wind even when rugged up & they seem to fall away to nothing in a very short time. The RA horses are now getting less work than usual owing to the more extensive employment of light railways but unfortunately the oat ration is reduced by 25% just at a time when food to keep up the body heat is most urgently required.	
	"		All evacuations of sick horses to Base stopped till further notice. This leaves the MVS with about 50 sick horses & delays the getting away of mange cases, which cannot be treated here under existing conditions.	
"	" 31		More snow, roads slippery in places & still a cutting N.E. wind. The last fortnight has been by far the most severe weather experienced during the campaign & is certain to increase the casualty returns of horses in the open. Materials for shelters & stables are very scarce & what with leave & sickness the number of men in wagon lines is much reduced. Watering is rather a difficulty owing to ice & the only good thing from the horse point of view is the absence of mud – this advantage is rather neutralised by lumpy frozen ground which constantly causes abrasions on the coronets.	98

[illegible] Major
ADVS 18 Div

Instructions regarding War Diaries and Intelligence Summaries are contained in F. S. Regs., Part II. and the Staff Manual respectively. Title Pages will be prepared in manuscript.

WAR DIARY
or
~~INTELLIGENCE SUMMARY~~
(Erase heading not required.)

Army Form C. 2118

ADVS/18D Vol 19

Place	Date	Hour	Summary of Events and Information	Remarks and references to Appendices
	1917		ADVS 18 Div VOL. 20.	
BOUZINCOURT	Feb. 1		Met DDVS at Mobile Vety Section	
	" 2		A2000 shews very heavy casualty return for this week – heavier than ever before. Nine horses in RA. have had to be destroyed for debility & exhaustion due to exposure. They became practically paralysed by the cold & reduced to such a state of weakness that unable to get up when they lay down. Nearly all from the same batch of remounts received at Xmas time & evidently recently discharged from V.H., having previously suffered from mange & debility. They have done very little work but are quite unable to stand the exposure to the cold & shrink away to nothing in two or three days.	
	" 6		Found B/84 horses looking very miserable in their lines which are on the side of a hill & very exposed to the North wind. Stabling is being built but progress very slow owing to difficulty in getting materials – during this dry cold weather wind screens are more important as they can be fixed up at once – wrote in to CRA. advising this & informing him that I had suggested it to OC B/84 wagon lines a week before but nothing done so far.	99

Instructions regarding War Diaries and Intelligence Summaries are contained in F. S. Regs., Part II. and the Staff Manual respectively. Title Pages will be prepared in manuscript.

WAR DIARY

~~or~~

~~INTELLIGENCE SUMMARY~~

(Erase heading not required.)

Army Form C. 2118

Place	Date 1917	Hour	Summary of Events and Information	Remarks and references to Appendices
BOUZINCOURT	Feb. 8.		Attended Conference at DDVS Office. Lt Cotton on leave to England – Capt Williams doing his work.	
"	" 9		Visited 150 Coy ASC. Good stabling built & horses looking the better for it. No signs of ulcerative stomatitis. Some very thin horses.	
"	" 10		Visited A/84 & D/83 & found cases of mange in each. Mange on the increase but impossible to clip out without stabling during this severe weather and quite out of the question to dress horses with a hot soln in the open ~~which~~ as it would be frozen on them before drying.	
"	" 12		Telephone conversation with DDVS. Evacuations are to be kept down as much as possible. Debility to be treated when possible in their lines & suspected mange clipped & dressed with Calcium sulphide soln to be prepared in M.V.S. I don't think there is much hope of doing debility cases any good in their lines whilst the present cold weather & shortage of forage continues. MVS evacuated 32 bad sarcoptic mange cases – this is the first lot evacuated since Jan. 27.	100

Army Form C. 2118.

Instructions regarding War Diaries and Intelligence Summaries are contained in F. S. Regs., Part II. and the Staff Manual respectively. Title pages will be prepared in manuscript.

WAR DIARY
or
INTELLIGENCE SUMMARY.
(Erase heading not required.)

Place	Date 1917	Hour	Summary of Events and Information	Remarks and references to Appendices
BOUZINCOURT	Feb 12		84 Bde becomes 84th Army Field Artillery Bde + D/84 divided up amongst 82 + 83 Bdes. Lt W R Cameron remains with 84th A F A Bde which is attached to 18 Div for time being	
	13		All R.A. units are affected with Mange. Sent C.R.A. a return of Mange cases which had occurred ~~since~~ during the last fortnight, for his information. I feel convinced that this mange could have been avoided to a very great extent limited if my advice to clip out all horses in the autumn had been followed + that it is the only way in which it can be kept down. Nothing less than an Army Order will ever cause this to be done.	
			31 Div Art attached to 18 Div temporarily. 3 AVC sergts reported from 31 Div + sent to M.V.S until posted.	
	16		Lt Cameron returned from leave having been held up at the Base owing to trains not running. ~~3 AVC sergts received from 31 Div.~~ Long spell of phenomenal frost broken. Rain today but still very cold.	
	17		Inspecting R.A. wagon lines to decide what cases of debility to evacuate + what can be treated in lines. Many cases have accumulated during the time evacuations could not go on as usual owing to railway difficulties + ~~[illegible]~~ congestion at the Base hospitals.	

101

A5834 Wt. W4973/M687 750,000 8/16 D. D. & L. Ltd. Forms/C.2118/13.

Instructions regarding War Diaries and Intelligence Summaries are contained in F. S. Regs., Part II. and the Staff Manual respectively. Title pages will be prepared in manuscript.

WAR DIARY

~~or~~

~~INTELLIGENCE SUMMARY.~~

(*Erase heading not required.*)

Army Form C. 2118.

Place	Date	Hour	Summary of Events and Information	Remarks and references to Appendices
	1917			
BOUZINCOURT	Feb 18		Very few debility cases are improving & most of them are getting worse which is only to be expected when food is short.	
			Sergt Brammall AVC sent to No 2 V.H. as surplus to establishment.	
	19		MVS steadily evacuating 4 trucks of horses three times a week, chiefly debility & mange. This is a higher percentage than the Division has ever had before.	
			Sent report from V.O. 83 Bde to HQ RA on horse on sick list for debility which was harnessed up & put in a team right down & had to be destroyed.	
	23		Inspected 150 Coy ASC & picked out seven debility cases for evacuation. The horses of this company have never had a chance to recover from the hardships of the early part of the winter & traffic precautions, which are now on, increase the normal work considerably. When delivering to battery wagon lines they usually have to pull through muddy fields for two or three hundred yards which takes it out of them more than two or three miles on a hard road.	
			Casualty returns very heavy this week, apart from those caused by shell fire.	102

A5834 Wt. W4973/M687 750,000 8/16 D. D. & L. Ltd. Forms/C.2118/13.

Instructions regarding War Diaries and Intelligence Summaries are contained in F. S. Regs., Part II. and the Staff Manual respectively. Title pages will be prepared in manuscript.

WAR DIARY

~~or~~

~~INTELLIGENCE~~ SUMMARY.

(Erase heading not required.)

Army Form C. 2118.

Place	Date	Hour	Summary of Events and Information	Remarks and references to Appendices
	1917			
BOUZINCOURT	Feb 23		V.O. 82 Bde reports case of debility horse being taken out to work & dying on road from exhaustion.	
	" 25		Wrote in to A.A.&Q.M.G. Remarks with copy of A2000 informing him of the two horses killed by R.A. by working them in an unfit state or sick list also suggesting that more care & supervision is necessary especially when horses are at work as they are frequently abused quite unnecessarily through ignorance & heedlessness. Copy to D.D.V.S. for information.	
	" 26		Guns moving forward – Some artillery teams out from 4 AM to 8 PM without getting watered. This of course is equal to a weeks work for horses that are on the thin side.	
			Lt Cotton reported his arrival from leave. Held up in England.	
			Reported to 18 D.V.A. my opinion that fit & active men are necessary for a Mobile Vety Section at the front, for various reasons.	103

Instructions regarding War Diaries and Intelligence Summaries are contained in F. S. Regs., Part II. and the Staff Manual respectively. Title pages will be prepared in manuscript.

WAR DIARY
~~or~~
~~INTELLIGENCE SUMMARY.~~
(Erase heading not required.)

Army Form C. 2118.

Place	Date 1917	Hour	Summary of Events and Information	Remarks and references to Appendices
BOUZINCOURT	Feb 28.		As regards artillery horses this month has been the worst the Division has had during the Campaign: Extraordinary severe weather, in the open – shortage of forage at a time when plenty was even more required to keep up the body heat & shortage of Remounts, which makes extra work for fit horses, when casualties are heavy & frequent.	
			Mange is much more prevalent than last year but few cases of Lousiness have been discovered. I think the cold has had an inhibiting effect on this & that lice will come later when the weather begins to improve.	
			Directly the weather becomes milder I shall advise the clipping of every horse as rapidly as possible & we may then be able to cope with these evils with some chance of success.	
			[illegible] Major A.D.V.S. 18 Div	104

A5834 Wt. W4973/M687 750,000 8/16 D. D. & L. Ltd. Forms/C.2118/13.

Instructions regarding War Diaries and Intelligence Summaries are contained in F. S. Regs., Part II. and the Staff Manual respectively. Title pages will be prepared in manuscript.

WAR DIARY
or
INTELLIGENCE SUMMARY.
(Erase heading not required.)

Army Form C. 2118.

ADVS 18 Division Vol 19/21

105

Place	Date 1917	Hour	Summary of Events and Information	Remarks and references to Appendices
			ADVS. 18. DIV VOL. 21.	
BOUZINCOURT	Mar 2		All RA wagon lines and Inf transports now located on E bank of ANCRE between Crucifix Corner & THIEPVAL	
	3		Wrote letter to DAQMG pointing out that at present rate of wastage the RA would be in danger of becoming immobile unless remounts can be supplied to make up strength wastage due to [illegible]. Wrote to DDVS my ideas as to advisability of reducing riding horses in MVS during existing state of trench warfare. Consider M.V.S could do without 10 Riders under present conditions but would want them again if forward movement took place. Consider also that MVS requires more transport either another limber or GS wagon or should not have to depend on horse float as transport, as, owing to its closeness to the ground it is apt to get stuck on heavy roads.	
	4		DHQ moved to Gough Huts X1 C 4 7 (D 57)	
	5		Inspected transport animals of 54 & 55 Inf Bdes – all animals looking extraordinary well	
	6		DDVS visited me & inspected No 4 Sec DAC.	

A5834 Wt. W4973/M687 750,000 8/16 D. D. & L. Ltd. Forms/C.2118/13.

Instructions regarding War Diaries and Intelligence Summaries are contained in F. S. Regs., Part II. and the Staff Manual respectively. Title pages will be prepared in manuscript.

WAR DIARY
or
INTELLIGENCE SUMMARY.
(Erase heading not required.)

Army Form C. 2118.

Place	Date 1917	Hour	Summary of Events and Information	Remarks and references to Appendices
Gough Huts	Mar. 7		Very cold wind	
			Visited RFA wagon lines – all in open but ground fairly good if rain keeps off.	
			Had telephone conversation with DDVS re carrying of ammunition for RA by pack. Expressed opinion that carrying packs caused animals to get more exhausted than drawing limbers although our animals have not been doing it long enough to quote any specific instances; the point about pack carrying is that when animals are held up by a block in the traffic they may have to stand for an hour or more still supporting the weight of the pack & cannot be relieved of it until the end of the journey is reached.	
	9		Attended Conference DDVS at Army HQ. Points discussed – debility cases & mange. MVS reduction of riders. MVS transport and Manage.	
			Attended Railhead from 8 pm till 2 am & issued 292 Remounts for DAQMG. Remounts generally good both as regards quality & condition. Mostly clipped & rugs provided from the train.	
	11		Arranged for Adv Collecting Post to be established by MVS at Q 24 D 2 9	
			Inspected 18 Div Train horses & wrote report to DDVS on same expressing opinion as to numbers requiring rest in lines & lighter work &c.	106

A5834 Wt. W4973/M687 750,000 8/16 D. D. & L. Ltd. Forms/C.2118/13.

Army Form C. 2118.

Instructions regarding War Diaries and Intelligence Summaries are contained in F. S. Regs., Part II. and the Staff Manual respectively. Title pages will be prepared in manuscript.

WAR DIARY
or
INTELLIGENCE SUMMARY.
(Erase heading not required.)

Place	Date 1916	Hour	Summary of Events and Information	Remarks and references to Appendices
Gough Huts	Nov. 12		M.V.S has now a good stock of Calcium sulphide made up & all V.Os are being supplied with what they require to dress suspected cases of mange & mud fever, very difficult to clip & dress in the open during cold & wet weather.	
	13		A/82 horses looking very poor & no doubt the pack carrying has exhausted them a great deal	
	15		Inspected Field Coy RE. Horses looking fairly well but have lost condition lately owing to overwork.	
	18		RA Wagon lines moved up to vicinity of IRLES.	
			MVS flooded with sick horses including some from 63 Div which is moving away. Visited MVS & arranged to send motor float to assist in collecting a number of cases unable to walk.	
			Sent in Report with A2000 on numbering of RA horses.	
	21		Motor horse float very useful to MVS & managed to get 13 cases to Railhead in time to box.	
	23		DHQ moved to DURY to entrain tomorrow at SALEUX for 1st Army Area.	
			RFA & 150 ASC marching down.	
STEENBECQUE	25		Arrived STEENBECQUE at 8 PM.	
	26		Visited DDVS 1st Army 7 PM in response to urgent telegram. Required information re condition of horses in 18 Div.	

Instructions regarding War Diaries and Intelligence Summaries are contained in F. S. Regs., Part II. and the Staff Manual respectively. Title pages will be prepared in manuscript.

WAR DIARY
or
INTELLIGENCE SUMMARY.
(Erase heading not required.)

Army Form C. 2118.

Place	Date 1917	Hour	Summary of Events and Information	Remarks and references to Appendices
STEENBECQUE	Mar. 27		Wrote Report to D.D.V.S. on condition of horses of Division send copy to A+Q for information	
"	28		M.V.S. arrived + billetted in farm No 48 on Morbecque – Neuville Rd.	
			A.D.V.S. i/c 53, 54 + 55 Inf Bdes for present + V.O. 18 Div Train i/c R.E.s + 54 + 55 F.A.	
			R.A. marching down due to arrive April 1st. V.O. with each Bde + one with D.A.C.	
			18 Div in G.H.Q. Reserve.	
			During the last two weeks the M.V.S. has been very heavily worked + evacuated regularly about 120 horses a week, except when evacuations were suspended. It has been necessary on two occasions to borrow [illegible] from units to assist in taking horses to railhead, which has never happened before. I consider great credit is due to the O.C. + all ranks for the satisfactory way in which the work has been carried on.	
			[illegible] Major, A.D.V.S. 18 Div	

108

Instructions regarding War Diaries and Intelligence Summaries are contained in F. S. Regs., Part II. and the Staff Manual respectively. Title pages will be prepared in manuscript.

WAR DIARY
or
INTELLIGENCE SUMMARY.
(Erase heading not required.)

Army Form C. 2118.

April 1917

ADVS 18 D

Vol 21

Place	Date	Hour	Summary of Events and Information	Remarks and references to Appendices
	1917		ADVS. 18. DIV. VOL. 22.	
STEENBECQUE	Apl. 1.		Attended conference of ADVS at DDVS office 1st Army H.Q. Subjects discussed – Extra men for M.V.S. during offensive operations – Railhead MVS & Corps M.V.S. Vety equipment – Debility cases. Mange	
	3		Visited Director of Railway Traffic at Hazebrouck re evacuating sick horses by rail, not feasible except from AIRE & LILLERS both of which rather too far. Best way will be by road to No. 23 V.H. St Omer (about 15 miles) and get loan of motor float from Army H.Q. if many to float	
	4		ADVS on leave to England till 14th. Capt. S.S. Gelbart officiating – to be recalled if the Division should undertake any active operations in meantime	
	16		ADVS returned to duty. Nothing of importance has happened but weather has been extraordinary severe for horses in the open – snowstorms & cutting N.E. winds – & consequently thin horses have not had any chance to improve in condition in spite of no work & extra attention.	
	17		Interviewed CRA with reference to condition of the horses of RA & the necessity for evacuating those whose condition was such that they would take three or four months to recover. Inspected C/83 with him & pointed out that a large number of the horses in this battery were unfit to bear any severe & sustained work at the present time. Evacuated 5 for debility & put several others on a thin line for special observation & no work whatever. Arranged to visit all units of RA with CRA.	

A5834 Wt. W4973 M687 750,000 8/16 D. D. & L. Ltd. Forms/C.2118/13.

Instructions regarding War Diaries and Intelligence Summaries are contained in F. S. Regs., Part II. and the Staff Manual respectively. Title pages will be prepared in manuscript.

WAR DIARY
or
~~INTELLIGENCE SUMMARY.~~

(*Erase heading not required.*)

Army Form C. 2118.

Place	Date 1917	Hour	Summary of Events and Information	Remarks and references to Appendices
STEENBECQUE	apl. 19		Inspected A/83 & B/83 with CRA & examined all debility cases not improving.	
			Borrowed Motor float from No 23 V.H to take four cases to hospital. Horses go in to the motor float much easier than into the horse float & travel more comfortably & altogether it is a most excellent conveyance.	
			Visited 152 Coy ASC & picked out 7 debility cases which must be evacuated. The Coy is moving tomorrow & is very short of horses but 4 quite unfit for the journey & will go to MVS tomorrow morning.	
	20		Inspected A/82 & B/82 with CRA. Both have improved during the last fortnight especially A/82 with the exception of a few mange & debility which will be evacuated.	
			Nearly all RA horses are lousy & CRA is against clipping during the cold weather. Explained to him the difficulty & danger of not clipping any lousy horse especially of rubbing his hair off & the chances of having mange as well which may not be detected until half the unit is ~~affected~~ infected. Advised him to leave it to the discretion of the V.O. &c. Undoubtedly thin horses lose condition if clipped in the cold weather unless they can be kept warm afterwards but this fact does not do away with the necessity for clipping in order to keep down contagious skin disease.	
	21		Inspected C/82 & D/82 with CRA.	110

A5834 Wt. W4973/M687 750,000 8/16 D. D. & L. Ltd. Forms/C.2118/13.

Army Form C. 2118.

Instructions regarding War Diaries and Intelligence Summaries are contained in F. S. Regs., Part II. and the Staff Manual respectively. Title pages will be prepared in manuscript.

WAR DIARY
~~or~~
INTELLIGENCE SUMMARY.

(*Erase heading not required.*)

Place	Date 1917	Hour	Summary of Events and Information	Remarks and references to Appendices
STEENBECQUE	Apl 22		Inspected B Echelon DAC & D/83.	
..	.. 23		Inspected with CRA No 1 & 2 Sec DAC. Horses & mules generally looking well.	
..	.. 24		RA moved to ~~G~~ GONNEHEM area.	
..	.. 25		Visited GONNEHEM Remount Rest Station and issued 62 Remounts (from CALAIS by road) for DAQ only	
PERNES	26		Marched to PERNES with DHQ. Rest of Division ~~to~~ to this area.	
HABARCQ	.. 27		Marched to HABARCQ with MVS.	
			18 Division ceased to belong to 1st Army at midday & became Third Army.	
AGNY	.. 28		Marched to AGNY with M.V.S.	
			Took over from ADVS 30 Div & No 30 M.V.S took over from No 40 MVS at AGNY CHATEAU.	
..	29		18 Div took over from 30 Div at midday.	
			Weather much improved dry & warmer.	

[illegible] Major
ADVS 18 Div

Instructions regarding War Diaries and Intelligence Summaries are contained in F. S. Regs., Part II. and the Staff Manual respectively. Title pages will be prepared in manuscript.

A.D.V.S.

May 1917

Vol 22

Army Form C. 2118.

WAR DIARY ~~or~~ INTELLIGENCE SUMMARY.

(Erase heading not required.)

Place	Date	Hour	Summary of Events and Information	Remarks and references to Appendices
	1917		ADVS. 18. DIV. VOL. 23.	
AGNY	May 1		Found RA & DAC – no animals left on march up. RA at BOIRY BECHERELLE	
	2		Established an ADV Collecting Post at N19 d 2 3 close to Sugar factory at NEUVILLE VITASSE	
			56 Div Art & 30 Div Art attached 18 Div for administration	
	8		Visited Railhead ARRAS to see MVS sick horses trucked.	
	9		Inspected Inf Bde transports – condition generally good.	
	10		Visited DAC & found many long animals which require clipping.	
			Wrote paper for DRO saying all horses to be clipped as soon as possible & sent to AA&QMG asking for insertion – All unit commanders talking nonsense about spoiling the summer coat by clipping as if anything could spoil the summer coat more than the ravages of lice not to mention the danger of concealing mange also.	
	11		Div Gas Officer gave demonstration to Transport Officers & others in adjusting the Anti gas respirator for horses. Held at MVS & all V.Os present.	112

A5834 Wt. W4973 M687 750,000 8/16 D. D. & L. Ltd. Forms/C.2118/13.

Instructions regarding War Diaries and Intelligence Summaries are contained in F. S. Regs., Part II. and the Staff Manual respectively. Title pages will be prepared in manuscript.

WAR DIARY
~~or~~
~~INTELLIGENCE SUMMARY.~~

(*Erase heading not required.*)

Army Form C. 2118.

Place	Date 1917	Hour	Summary of Events and Information	Remarks and references to Appendices
AGNY	May 12		Interviewed Divisional Commander re my request to have all horses clipped & gave him my reasons for same, which he agreed to consider.	
"	15		D.H.Q. moved to S17 a 8 4 (57B) Recalled ADV Collecting Post. Rode out with OC MVS to find a site for Section. attended Conference at DDVS Office.	
S17 a 8.4	16		Moved my office to S17 a 8 4.	
"	17		MVS moved to near DHQ S16 A 4.8 (57B) Infantry & RA lines close by	
"	18		RA rest camp for thin horses established under supervision of attached Cavalry Officers. Excellent grazing & thin horses will have a complete rest & plenty of food.	
"	24		Assisted DAQMG in issuing 140 Remounts for the Division. All horses improving owing to good weather, moderate work & excellent grazing also have persuaded units to clip off all the old ragged coats so that no valuable time will be wasted in putting animals under best possible conditions. Several cases of mange have been discovered as a result of this clipping & practically all shew signs of lice dermatitis.	113

A5834 Wt. W4973/M687 750,000 8/16 D. D. & L. Ltd. Forms/C.2118/13.

Instructions regarding War Diaries and Intelligence Summaries are contained in F. S. Regs., Part II. and the Staff Manual respectively. Title pages will be prepared in manuscript.

WAR DIARY

~~or~~

INTELLIGENCE ~~SUMMARY~~.

(Erase heading not required.)

Army Form C. 2118.

Place	Date 1917	Hour	Summary of Events and Information	Remarks and references to Appendices
S17A8.4	May 30		Many cases of a specific form of Ophthalmia have occurred recently, the cause of which is somewhat obscure – the whole of the eye is affected & recovery takes from a fortnight to three weeks. Am advising the isolation & segregation of all cases.	
"	31		Sent in report to DDR re my opinion of various types of animals used in the field as regards their stamina & lasting power which type is recommended to try & breed. Recommend the heavy weight hunter type as the most useful all round animal.	
			ADVS & OC 30 MVS received a mention in recent despatches.	
			The horses of the Division have ~~[illegible]~~ never had such an opportunity to recuperate as in this area and are all improving daily in condition	
			ASC have had a good deal of unnecessary work owing to ARRAS being railhead but this is being changed tomorrow.	
			[signature] ADVS 18 Div	

114

A5834 Wt. W4973/M687 750,000 8/16 D. D. & L. Ltd. Forms/C.2118/13.

Instructions regarding War Diaries and Intelligence Summaries are contained in F. S. Regs., Part II. and the Staff Manual respectively. Title pages will be prepared in manuscript.

WAR DIARY
or
INTELLIGENCE SUMMARY.
(*Erase heading not required.*)

Army Form C. 2118.

ADVS 18 D
Vol 23

Place	Date 1917	Hour	Summary of Events and Information	Remarks and references to Appendices
			ADVS. 18. DIV VOL. 24.	
S17A8.4	June 3.		Attended Conference of DDVS at 3rd Army H.Q. - subjects discussed, weekly returns, Corps ADVS, Mange.	
	" 9		Had consultation with cavalry officer attached to Corps H.Q. for horsemastership.	
	" 11		18 Signal Coy horses & those attached tested with mallein (intra dermic) owing to their propinquity to an affected Heavy Battery.	
	" 12		Inspected Signal Coy horses malleined yesterday - no reactions.	
	" 13		Inspected Signal Coy horses malleined on 11th - no reactions.	
	" 14		ADVS VII Corps visited Mobile Vety Section.	
COUIN	" 18		D.H.Q. moved to COUIN. Inf Bdes to same area. Capt Austin from 83 Bde marched with M.V.S for temporary duty. Capt Williams & Lt Cotton remain with 18 Div Art which is attached to 50. Div ~~[illegible]~~ in forward area. Capt Austin i/c 53, 54 & 55 Inf Bdes. Capt Macdougall i/c 18 Div Train (less Coy) R.E. & Fd Ambulances.	15

A5834 Wt. W4973/M687 750,000 8/16 D. D. & L. Ltd. Forms/C.2118/13.

Instructions regarding War Diaries and Intelligence Summaries are contained in F. S. Regs., Part II. and the Staff Manual respectively. Title pages will be prepared in manuscript.

WAR DIARY

~~or~~

~~INTELLIGENCE SUMMARY.~~

(Erase heading not required.)

Army Form C. 2118.

Place	Date	Hour	Summary of Events and Information	Remarks and references to Appendices
	1917			
COUIN	June 22		Visited No 22 V.H. with DAQMG.	
"	" 23		Capt E.S. Gilbert on leave to ENGLAND. Capt Austin i/c MVS.	
"	" 30		Very little sickness this month & few evacuations. All horses & mules much improved in condition owing to favourable weather, plentiful grazing & not too much work.	

[illegible signature]
ADVS 18 Div

116

A5834 Wt. W4973/M687 750,000 8/16 D. D. & L. Ltd. Forms/C.2118/13.

Instructions regarding War Diaries and Intelligence Summaries are contained in F. S. Regs., Part II. and the Staff Manual respectively. Title pages will be prepared in manuscript.

WAR DIARY
or
INTELLIGENCE SUMMARY.
(Erase heading not required.)

DADOS 18th Div.
June 1917.
Vol 23

Army Form C. 2118.

Place	Date 1917	Hour	Summary of Events and Information	Remarks and references to Appendices
Boisleux au Mont	June 1		Divisional Employment Coy arrived - No. 21.	
	2		Railhead shelled. Lorry with load of horse shoes, badly damaged.	
	8		Both drivers & 1 attached man wounded, one driver severely. Ptes Eames & English (attached) admitted to Hospital, with slight wound & shell shock respectively. Former returned to duty same day.	
	9		Moved 56 Div Arty to 21 Div:-	
			" 14 Div Arty, 50 Div Arty & 181 Tunnelling Coy from 14 Div.	
	16		" all above to 50 Div.	
Couin	17		Moved Stores & Office to Couin.	
	22		" 8 Royal Sussex Pioneers to 30 Div.	
			80 Field Coy " do.	
			79 do " 8 Div.	
			92 do " II Corps Troops.	
			" CRE " do.	
	24		After moving to Couin continuing to administer 18 RA. Sending one or two lorries to [illegible] R.P. about twice a week.	
	28		After this date no stores being dispatched from Base (Havre) owing instructions. Units to be notified by me when ready to receive them.	

[illegible] Lieut
DADOS 18 Div.

17

Instructions regarding War Diaries and Intelligence Summaries are contained in F. S. Regs., Part II. and the Staff Manual respectively. Title pages will be prepared in manuscript.

WAR DIARY

or

~~INTELLIGENCE SUMMARY.~~

(Erase heading not required.)

Army Form C. 2118.

DADVS 18 D

Vol 24

Place	Date 1917	Hour	Summary of Events and Information	Remarks and references to Appendices
			DADVS. 18. Div Vol. 25.	
COUIN	July 1		Appointment of ADVS to Corps comes into force from today with temporary rank of Lt Col. ADVS Division becomes DADVS. All returns to go through ADVS Corps instead of direct to DDVS	
DOULLENS	" 3		DHQ marched to DOULLENS and billetted for night	
STEENVORDE	" 4		Entrained 6 am. and arrived STEENVORDE 2 PM.	
"	" 5		M.V.S located HOPOUTRE. Capt JELBART returned from leave. Division concentrated in II Corps area less Div Art marching up.	
RENINGHELST	" 7		Marched to RENINGHELST and took over office & billet vacated by DADVS. 30 Div called to see ADVS II Corps.	
"	" 9		Visited DICKEBUSCH to pick site for MVS adv Collecting Post and arranged to establish same tomorrow	
"	" 12		18 Div Art arrived in area marching from S of Arras & wagon lines located west of DICKEBUSCH. a good march up only three animals left on the way and all looking well.	118

A5834 Wt. W4973/M687 750,000 8/16 D. D. & L. Ltd. Forms/C.2118/13.

Instructions regarding War Diaries and Intelligence Summaries are contained in F. S. Regs., Part II. and the Staff Manual respectively. Title pages will be prepared in manuscript.

Army Form C. 2118.

WAR DIARY
or
~~INTELLIGENCE SUMMARY.~~
(*Erase heading not required.*)

Place	Date	Hour	Summary of Events and Information	Remarks and references to Appendices
	1917			
RENINGHELST	July 14.		Attended conference at ADVS office II Corps.	
			Attended conference at AA&QMG's office re arrangements for offensive.	
..	.. 15		Visited 150 CRASC to see 30 horses gassed last night by gas shells. One killed in extremis. P.M. extensive oedema of lungs which were much enlarged and pale in colour. Blood very black and tarry. This horse was apparently alright until taken to assist in pulling a wagon out of a ditch – he soon after developed most acute symptoms of distress and dyspnoea & was shot when throwing himself about. Two others are blowing very badly, the remainder beyond an occasional cough are not distressed. Treatment Inhalations of oxygen for the badly affected the others to remain on the line & not to be moved even for watering. All eventually recovered. Gas helmets were not put on owing to excessive shelling & necessity to get away as soon as possible. Oxygen had an excellent effect where used but difficult to obtain.	119

Instructions regarding War Diaries and Intelligence Summaries are contained in F. S. Regs., Part II. and the Staff Manual respectively. Title pages will be prepared in manuscript.

WAR DIARY

~~or~~

~~INTELLIGENCE SUMMARY.~~

(Erase heading not required.)

Army Form C. 2118.

Place	Date 1917	Hour	Summary of Events and Information	Remarks and references to Appendices
RENINGHELST	July 16.		First batch of sick horses sent to Corps Mob Vet Det situated near railhead (WIPPENHOEK) and ~~[illegible]~~ formed by taking four men from each Mob Vet Sec. This area is very difficult for evacuations of sick as empty supply trains are not utilised and cases which cannot travel by road to St OMER have to wait until a special train is requisitioned by DDVS. Daily casualties from shell fire are very heavy and unless trains are supplied frequently & regularly mobile sections become congested.	
"	20.		Sent Sergt and 1 man to stop at ADV Collecting Post & accompany police patrol in forward area to destroy or collect wounded & abandoned horses. During the last week over 50 horses of RA. have been killed by shellfire when taking up ammunition at night.	
"	" 21		13 horses gassed by gas shells, belonging to D.A.C – no deaths.	
"	" 22		DDVS Fifth Army visited 30 MVS.	120

A5834 Wt. W4973/M687 750,000 8/16 D. D. & L. Ltd. Forms/C.2118/13.

Instructions regarding War Diaries and Intelligence Summaries are contained in F. S. Regs., Part II. and the Staff Manual respectively. Title pages will be prepared in manuscript.

WAR DIARY
~~or~~
~~INTELLIGENCE SUMMARY.~~
(Erase heading not required.)

Army Form C. 2118.

Place	Date 1917	Hour	Summary of Events and Information	Remarks and references to Appendices
RENINGHELST	July 24		Accompanied DAQMG to PROVEN to issue 121 Remounts arriving by rail. OC 30 MVS detailed by ADVS II Corps to attend at Railhead & assist in entraining horses from CMVD by special train.	
"	" 27		Signal Co horselines bombed at night 33 horses killed & 32 wounded also No 7 Sec DAC where 22 were killed & 12 wounded	
"	" 29		Capt PJ Austin returned from leave & detailed to go to No 9 V.H. for duty as such Division is being reduced by one V.O. – this leaves only 4 V.Os besides the DADVS including one with the MVS, which will make it very difficult to carry on the Vety duties properly & some units are bound to suffer from want of attention. At the same time it is proposed to reduce the V.Os attached to RA Bdes to 1 charger which in my opinion is absolutely wrong for if any man in a Division requires two chargers it is a V.O. who is entirely dependent on his horses.	
"	" 30		Wrote in to DAQMG & ADVS II Corps protesting against the taking away of 1 charger from the RA V.Os. The casualties this month have been very heavy due to the number of animals killed & wounded by shell fire.	121
			[signature] Major DADVS 28 Div	

A5834 Wt. W4973/M687 750,000 8/16 D. D. & L. Ltd. Forms/C.2118/13.

Instructions regarding War Diaries and Intelligence Summaries are contained in F. S. Regs., Part II. and the Staff Manual respectively. Title pages will be prepared in manuscript.

WAR DIARY ~~or~~ ~~INTELLIGENCE SUMMARY.~~

(Erase heading not required.)

D.A.D.V.S. 18th Divn

Vol 25

Army Form C. 2118.

Place	Date 1917	Hour	Summary of Events and Information	Remarks and references to Appendices
			DADVS 18 Div Vol. 26	
REMINGHELST	Aug 1		Capt P. J. AUSTIN left the Division to go to No. 9 V.H. in accordance with instructions received. Lt Cotton attached to 83 Bde RFA.	
			Heavy rain making horse lines bad & increasing the hardships of taking up ammunition &c.	
..	.. 4		Attended Conference at Office of ADVS II Corps, nothing of importance discussed.	
			Attended PROVEN railhead & issued 129 Remounts for DAQMG.	
..	.. 8		Some of the RA horses are beginning to shew loss of condition especially in the howitzer batteries where double journeys have to be made to take up the same amount of ammunition as the 18 pounders get in one journey.	
			Many cases of severe injury to feet & coronets are occurring daily owing to the bad condition of the corduroy road – also many cases of pricked feet from picked-up-nail from stepping on shoes with nails in them which had been torn off by the corduroy road. Drew attention of Q to this.	122

A5834 Wt. W4973/M687 750,000 8/16 D. D. & L. Ltd. Forms/C.2118/13.

Instructions regarding War Diaries and Intelligence Summaries are contained in F. S. Regs., Part II. and the Staff Manual respectively. Title pages will be prepared in manuscript.

WAR DIARY
or
INTELLIGENCE SUMMARY.
(Erase heading not required.)

Army Form C. 2118.

Place	Date	Hour	Summary of Events and Information	Remarks and references to Appendices
	1917			
RENINGHELST	Aug. 9		Visited 113 AFA Bde & wrote report to ADVS II Corps on condition of horses in D Bty. Many very debilitated require evacuating.	
"	" 10		ADV Post doing a lot of work & getting horses from three or four different Div Arty – MVS also very full.	
"	" 11		77 sick horses in MVS at 6.30 P.M.	
"	" 12		Attended Conference at office of ADVS II Corps. Urged the necessity for more frequent train service in order to avoid getting the Mobile Vet Section clogged up.	
"	" 13		II Corps order saying that all horses to be clipped between mid September & end of October & after that trace high only. This is an excellent idea if only the clipping machines are issued early enough to enable it to be done. Wrote ADVS II Corps pointing this out & suggesting they should be issued at once.	
"	" 14		As the Division moves back to rest tomorrow withdrew ADV Post today with much trouble owing to the number of cases needing the float. DADVS 56 Division assisted me by floating two cases to his MVS.	123

*A5834 Wt. W4973/M687 750,000 8/16 D. D. & L. Ltd. Forms/C.2118/13.

Army Form C. 2118.

WAR DIARY
or
INTELLIGENCE SUMMARY.
(Erase heading not required.)

Instructions regarding War Diaries and Intelligence Summaries are contained in F. S. Regs., Part II. and the Staff Manual respectively. Title pages will be prepared in manuscript.

Place	Date 1917	Hour	Summary of Events and Information	Remarks and references to Appendices
LEDERZEELE	Aug. 15.		DHQ moved to LEDERZEELE and Inf Bdes into surrounding area. RA remaining in line & Capt Wilkins & Lt Cotton with them. MVS to hand over train cases to CMVD today & evacuate road cases & to march done tomorrow. Arranged to send 3 men back to report to DADVS 56 Div for duty as his MVS will be evacuating horses from 18 Div Art. This should always be done as a general rule when the RA of a Division remain behind in the line especially when casualties are heavy.	
"	" 16		MVS located at LES CINQ RUES close to Ledezeele.	
"	" 18		Attended conference at office of ADVS VIII Corps between ADVS & myself as only my Division at present in the Corps. Nothing of importance discussed.	
"	" 20		Allotment of Vety duties in back area.	
			Major Harvey — DHQ & 53 Inf Bde & attached units	
			Capt Holland — 54 Inf Bde	
			Capt Macdougall — ASC. REs FAs & 55 Inf Bde.	
			All of above units in pretty good order & few casualties, which is fortunate as the area is very wide.	124

A5834 Wt. W4973 M687 750,000 8/16 D. D. & L. Ltd. Forms/C.2118/13.

Army Form C. 2118.

Instructions regarding War Diaries and Intelligence Summaries are contained in F. S. Regs., Part II. and the Staff Manual respectively. Title pages will be prepared in manuscript.

WAR DIARY
or
~~INTELLIGENCE SUMMARY.~~

(Erase heading not required.)

Place	Date 1917	Hour	Summary of Events and Information	Remarks and references to Appendices
LEDERZEELE	Augst		Capt J. L. WILLIAMS on leave to England – Lt Cotton doing his work	
"	" 24		Accompanied ADVS & Corps Horse Master VIII Corps in inspection of mares for breeding purposes. Very few branded.	
"	" 25		Capt W.F. MACDOUGALL reported wounded whilst visiting his battery in forward area & taken to No 23 C.C.S.	
"	" 26		Capt Macdougall evacuated to No 20. ~~Station~~ Hospital. Wired ADVS for a relief. Capt [illegible] & myself dividing the vety work of the Division between us.	
"	" 30		Division joined V Corps at midday.	
"	" 31		Visited ADVS V Corps in response to telegram received last night & am detailed to visit No 2 & 4 Sick Horse Halts. 18 Div Art moved back from line to rest at OUDERZEELE.	

[signature] Major
DADVS 18 Div.

125

A5834 Wt. W4973/M687 750,000 8/16 D. D. & L. Ltd. Forms/C.2118/13.

Instructions regarding War Diaries and Intelligence Summaries are contained in F. S. Regs., Part II. and the Staff Manual respectively. Title pages will be prepared in manuscript.

11

WAR DIARY
or
~~INTELLIGENCE SUMMARY.~~

(Erase heading not required.)

DADVS

Vol 26

Army Form C. 2118.

Place	Date	Hour	Summary of Events and Information	Remarks and references to Appendices
	1917		~~DADVS~~ 18 Div VOL No 27	
LEDERZEELE	Sept. 1		18 Div Art moved to OUDERZEELE to rest.	
ESQUELBEC	" 3		D.H.Q. & my office moved to ESQUELBEC. Capt Williams returned from leave.	
"	" 4		30 MVS moved to ESQUELBEC.	
"	" 6		Lt Cotton on leave to England.	
"	" 7		Lieut N. BISSET reported for duty vice Capt W.F. MACDOUGALL & attached to 18 Div Train.	
"	" 8		Visited RFA Brigades – horses generally looking fairly well considering the hard time they have had. A few cases to be evacuated for Debility.	
"	" 11		Visited D.A.C. Pinned Remounts for D.A.Q.M.G.	
"	" 16		Sent in Recommendations for New Year Honours as under –	
			Capt E.E. JELBART M.C.	
			" J.L. WILLIAMS mention in despatches	
			" P.J. AUSTIN " "	
			" W.F. MACDOUGALL " "	
			Sergt T. THORNLEY M.S.M.	126

A5834 Wt. W4973 M687 750,000 8/16 D. D. & L. Ltd. Forms/C.2118/13.

Army Form C. 2118.

Instructions regarding War Diaries and Intelligence Summaries are contained in F. S. Regs., Part II. and the Staff Manual respectively. Title pages will be prepared in manuscript.

WAR DIARY
~~or~~
~~INTELLIGENCE SUMMARY.~~
(*Erase heading not required.*)

Place	Date 1917	Hour	Summary of Events and Information	Remarks and references to Appendices
ESQUELBEC	Sept 20		Visited ADVS XVIII Corps re moving into his area shortly & to find site for 30 MVS.	
..	.. 21		DADVS on ten days leave to England. Capt Gelland to officiate.	
..	.. 23		30 MVS moved to F 28 b 1.4 ~~to~~ POPERINGHE area.	
POPERINGHE	.. 24		DHQ moved to POPERINGHE into XVIII Corps.	
..	.. 25		18 Div Art moved into forward area and took over from 48 Div Art. Wagon lines situated west of VLAMERTINGHE	
..	.. 26		30 MVS evacuates through Corps M.V. Det at PROVEN, where sick horses are put on train. Sick Horse Halts have been closed down. Evacuation by rail is much to be preferred from every point of view when a long distance from the receiving hospital. Have got a D.R.O. published ordering all horses & mules to be clipped as quickly as possible. The clipping of mules has since been forbidden by G.R.O. — on what grounds I am unable to understand. My experience last year of mules which were clipped in October was that they kept extraordinary well & healthy during the winter. [illegible] Major DADVS 18 Div	127

A5834 Wt. W4973/M687 750,000 8/16 D. D. & L. Ltd. Forms/C.2118/13.

16

Instructions regarding War Diaries and Intelligence Summaries are contained in F. S. Regs., Part II. and the Staff Manual respectively. Title pages will be prepared in manuscript.

WAR DIARY
or
INTELLIGENCE SUMMARY.
(Erase heading not required.)

DADVS 18 D
Vol 27

Army Form C. 2118.

Place	Date	Hour	Summary of Events and Information	Remarks and references to Appendices
	1917		DADVS. 18 Div Vol No 28	
POPERINGHE	Oct 2.		DADVS returned from leave to England.	
..	.. 6		attended XVIII Corps HQ conference with ADVS.	
			Visited Railhead & issued 20 Remounts for HQ mly.	
			Visited DADVS 11 Div re Taking over from his MVS when we relieve them.	
..	.. 7		Lt N. BISSET on leave to England.	
..	.. 10		Visited KEMPTON PARK with OC MVS to pick site for an Adv Dressing Station when the offensive takes place.	
Border Camp	.. 11		DHQ moved to BORDER CAMP	
			MVS to A28 a 8.9 & took over from 11 Div MVS who left 31 horses with several [illegible] cases.	
			Advd Post for dressing wounded animals established at C15 B (KEMPTON PARK)	128

A5834 Wt. W4973 M687 750,000 8/16 D. D. & L. Ltd. Forms/C.2118/13.

WAR DIARY

~~or~~

~~INTELLIGENCE SUMMARY.~~

(*Erase heading not required.*)

Instructions regarding War Diaries and Intelligence Summaries are contained in F. S. Regs., Part II. and the Staff Manual respectively. Title pages will be prepared in manuscript.

Army Form C. 2118.

Place	Date 1917	Hour	Summary of Events and Information	Remarks and references to Appendices
BORDER CAMP	Oct. 13.		To ADVS office XVIII Corps. advised the issue of 15% of strength horse rugs which will be sufficient to put on recently clipped & sick animals as weather has got much colder rather suddenly.	
"	" 14		Visited RA wagon lines – majority of horses looking fairly well but howitzer battery horses losing condition owing to extra work they always have to do in taking up ammunition. MVS very congested chiefly by animals from attached RA units & Corps collecting station being frequently closed & unable to take animals in for evacuation. The arrangement of Corps Collecting Station is not satisfactory & does not appear to be able to cope with the very heavy increase in casualties caused by the nightly bombing which takes a huge toll of animals owing to the congestion of horse lines in the area.	129

A5834 Wt. W4973 M687 750,000 8/16 D. D. & L. Ltd. Forms/C.2118/13.

Army Form C. 2118.

Instructions regarding War Diaries and Intelligence Summaries are contained in F. S. Regs., Part II. and the Staff Manual respectively. Title pages will be prepared in manuscript.

WAR DIARY
~~or~~
~~INTELLIGENCE SUMMARY.~~
(Erase heading not required.)

Place	Date	Hour	Summary of Events and Information	Remarks and references to Appendices
	1917			
BORDER CAMP	Oct 20		To ADVS office XVIII Corps.	
POPERINGHE	" 25		DHQ moved to POPERINGHE being relieved by 58 Div. RA & Sussex Pioneers attached to 58 DIV, MVS remaining as before.	
	" 27		To ADVS office XVIII Corps. Received instructions from ADVS 14th Corps that when we move into their area 30 MVS will act as VCCS for 14th Corps. Took order to "Q" who will protest against MVS being taken away from the ~~Division~~.	
PROVEN	30		DHQ moved to PROVEN into XIX Corps area (XIX Corps having relieved 14th Corps) MVS to A14 B8.3 to act as V.C.C.S.	
	31		Visited MVS at A14 B8.3 & found it had taken over 200 horses for evacuation from the MVS of 34 Div which had previously been acting as a VCCS for the whole of the two Corps. This in my opinion is a bad precedent & it should not be possible for the ADVS of a Corps to take away any M.V.S from its ~~Division~~ to act as a V.C.C.S. which ought to be a separate & additional unit.	130

[illegible] Major
DADVS. 18 Div

A5834 Wt. W4973/M687 750,000 8/16 D. D. & L. Ltd. Forms/C.2118/13.

17

Instructions regarding War Diaries and Intelligence Summaries are contained in F. S. Regs., Part II. and the Staff Manual respectively. Title pages will be prepared in manuscript.

WAR DIARY

~~or~~ ~~INTELLIGENCE SUMMARY.~~

(*Erase heading not required.*)

Army Form C. 2118.

DADVS 18 D

Vol 28

Place	Date	Hour	Summary of Events and Information	Remarks and references to Appendices
	1917		DADVS 18 DIV Vol 29	
PROVEN	Nov. 1		Visited MVS acting as V.C.C.S & congested with horses which they cannot evacuate fast enough owing to not having sufficient men to send down the line. In my opinion the whole scheme is a bad muddle & if it is desired to have a VCCS it should be a separate unit extra to mobile vety sections which cannot be spared from their Divisions.	
	4		Wrote a letter to ADVS XIX Corps protesting against my MVS being taken to act as a VCCS for various reasons and suggesting that if a VCCS cannot be formed as a separate and extra unit it would be far more satisfactory for mobile sections to each do their own work each having an equal number of the extra men from the base. Asked him to forward this letter to higher authority & send copy of same to A A & QMG for information	
J Camp	5		HQ moved to J Camp A 14 B.15.	
	6		Attended conference at ADVS Corps H.Q. at which DDVS was present	3

A5834 Wt. W4973/M687 750,000 8/16 D. D. & L. Ltd. Forms/C.2118/13.

Instructions regarding War Diaries and Intelligence Summaries are contained in F. S. Regs., Part II. and the Staff Manual respectively. Title pages will be prepared in manuscript.

WAR DIARY
or
INTELLIGENCE SUMMARY.
(Erase heading not required.)

Army Form C. 2118.

Place	Date	Hour	Summary of Events and Information	Remarks and references to Appendices
	1917			
J Camp	Nov. 6		DDVS agreed with my letter & suggestions & it was arranged that each MVS should evacuate its own horses with the exception that No. 30 MVS being near Railhead should take in all the float cases from the other mobile sections & have the Motor Ambulance on evacuation days to get them to the train.	
"	" 9		Visited Railhead & assisted OC 30 MVS to get 273 horses into the train to clear up the VCCS. Borrowed ten men from RA through Q to enable us to send this number down. After today each OC MVS will arrange to put his own horses on the train, which will be far more satisfactory as it is infinitely easier for one man to entrain 70 or 80 animals than two or three hundred.	
"	" 11		DHQ moved to ELVERDINGHE Chateau my office remaining for the present at J Camp. Visited PROVEN railhead & received 120 Remounts for [illegible].	132

A5834 Wt. W4973/M687 750,000 8/16 D. D. & L. Ltd. Forms/C.2118/13.

Army Form C. 2118.

Instructions regarding War Diaries and Intelligence Summaries are contained in F. S. Regs., Part II. and the Staff Manual respectively. Title pages will be prepared in manuscript.

WAR DIARY
or
~~INTELLIGENCE~~ SUMMARY.

(Erase heading not required.)

Place	Date	Hour	Summary of Events and Information	Remarks and references to Appendices
	1917			
I Camp	NOV. 12		The chief trouble in evacuating, when casualties are heavy from bombing & shellfire, is shortage of men to go down to the base when one man has to go with each truck. One can cope with this more or less when empty supply trucks can be utilised daily but when, as in this area, only special trains can be used, & these for not less than 200 horses, a Mobile Vety Section has not got the men & is obliged to get assistance from other sources. What is really required in an area like this is an advanced hospital capable of dealing with a thousand or fifteen hundred animals close enough up for walking cases to reach it by road & others to be floated from Mobile Vety Sections.	
"	15		There is a noticeable improvement in the general condition of the majority of animals as compared with this time last year especially in the heavy draught horses and I attribute this largely to the more generous hay diet which has been issued lately & also to the more extensive use of chaff machines. The few extra pounds of hay to the daily diet has made an extraordinary difference to the condition of the H.D.	133

A5834 Wt. W4973 M687 750,000 8/16 D. D. & L. Ltd. Forms/C.2118/13.

Army Form C. 2118.

Instructions regarding War Diaries and Intelligence Summaries are contained in F. S. Regs., Part II. and the Staff Manual respectively. Title pages will be prepared in manuscript.

WAR DIARY
or
INTELLIGENCE SUMMARY.
(Erase heading not required.)

Place	Date	Hour	Summary of Events and Information	Remarks and references to Appendices
	1917			
ELVERDINGHE	Nov 22		Moved my office to ELVERDINGHE Chateau. Withdrew ADV Dressing Post which has had practically no animals during the last week & means a loss of two men from the M.V.S.	
	24		Sergt A. AMESBURY arrived to 53 Inf Bde vice Sergt BARRETT evacuated sick	
	30		There has been very little cold weather during the month & the chief things horses have had to contend with have been bombs & mud – casualties have been numerous from the former. Mange has been conspicuous by its absence & this is probably largely due to more clipping having been done than last year.	

[signature] Major
DADVS 18 Div

134

A5834 Wt. W4973/M687 750,000 8/16 D. D. & L. Ltd. Forms/C.2118/13.

Army Form C. 2118.

DADVS 18 D
Vol 29

Instructions regarding War Diaries and Intelligence Summaries are contained in F. S. Regs., Part II. and the Staff Manual respectively. Title pages will be prepared in manuscript.

WAR DIARY
or
~~INTELLIGENCE SUMMARY.~~
(Erase heading not required.)

Place	Date	Hour	Summary of Events and Information	Remarks and references to Appendices
	1917		DADVS 18 Div Vol. 30	
ELVERDINGHE	Decr 3		Attended conference ADVS office XIX Corps – nothing of importance discussed. Interviewed A/Staff Sergt WARSOP in presence of O.C. 30 M.V.S. & pointed out to him the necessity of his acquiring proficiency in the management of the office & rendition of returns &c if he is to give his O.C. the assistance he requires in order to free him for outside work. Apparently this N.C.O. has never had any training in office work or returns before being promoted to Staff Sergt which seems rather extraordinary. In my opinion this is what is chiefly required in a staff sergeant for a M.V.S. as one rarely finds a man in the rest of the personnel who is sufficiently educated to assist in the at times quite large amount of writing which has to be done.	
	6		On instructions from ADVS Corps picked out a site for establishing an adv collecting or aid post should such be considered necessary. B.10 C 2 3 Sheet 28	135

A5834 Wt. W4973/M687 750,000 8/16 D. D. & L. Ltd. Forms/C.2118/13.

Instructions regarding War Diaries and Intelligence Summaries are contained in F. S. Regs., Part II. and the Staff Manual respectively. Title pages will be prepared in manuscript.

WAR DIARY
or
~~INTELLIGENCE SUMMARY.~~

(Erase heading not required.)

Army Form C. 2118.

Place	Date 1917	Hour	Summary of Events and Information	Remarks and references to Appendices
ELVERDINGHE	Dec 7		Capt E.E. Gellard on leave to England till 21.12.17 – Lt Bird to take charge of No 30 MVS during his absence & DADVS to do Lt Bird's work.	
	8		attended Conference at ADVS office XIX Corps.	
			DADVS clerk on leave to England till 22.12.17	
	12		18 Div Art moved out of line to CROMBEKE area for a much needed rest.	
ROUSBRUGGE	18		D.H.Q. moved to ROUSBRUGGE. 30 MVS to PROVEN E12 d 3.9 (Sheet 27) being relieved by 2/1 W.L. MVS (57 Div). 53 & 54 Bdes in same area. 55 Bde to NORDAUSQUE.	
	22		visited 55 Bde & 153 Coy ASC at NORDAUSQUE with S.S.O.	
			Capt H.L. WILLIAMS on leave to England	
	23		Capt E.E. Gellard arrived back from leave.	
	29		attended conference ADVS office XIX Corps.	
			Weather severe & roads very slippery. Horses generally looking pretty well & very little sickness.	
			Capt H.L. Williams "mentioned" in despatches.	136

[illegible] Major
DADVS. 18 Div

A5834 Wt. W4973 M687 750,000 8/16 D. D. & L. Ltd. Forms/C.2118/13.

Army Form C. 2118.

11

Instructions regarding War Diaries and Intelligence Summaries are contained in F. S. Regs., Part II. and the Staff Manual respectively. Title pages will be prepared in manuscript.

WAR DIARY
or
~~INTELLIGENCE SUMMARY.~~
(Erase heading not required.)

DADVS 18 D
Vol 30

Place	Date	Hour	Summary of Events and Information	Remarks and references to Appendices
	1918		DADVS. 18. Div. Vol. 31	
ROUSBRUGGE	Jan 3		D.H.Q. moved to ELVERDINGHE Chateau. No 30 MVS to A3 C 1.4 (Sheet 28) Taking over from MVS of 57 Division. Roads very slippery from frozen snow & frost cogs much in request	
ELVERDINGHE	4		Visited Corps HQ to see ADVS re taking over his charge whilst on leave – to remain at D.H.Q. (telephonic communication) & visit Corps every other day unless necessary to do so more frequently.	
	5		Inspected Remounts at HQ DAC for D.H.Q. Units. LDs good, Riders bad.	
	6		Accompanied AA&QMG in a tour of inspection of 1st Line Transports 53 & 55 Inf Bdes – all looking well except 8th R Berks, who have several thin horses.	
			New Year Honours – DADVS, DSO – OC 30 MVS, M.C. – Sergt. T. THORNLEY 30 MVS. MSM	
	7		Capt J.L. Williams returned from leave from England.	
	8		Capt S.J. Cotton proceeded on leave to England.	
			Weather very severe frost & snow – roads very slippery for horse transport	137

A5834 Wt. W4973/M687 750,000 8/16 D. D. & L. Ltd. Forms/C.2118/13.

Instructions regarding War Diaries and Intelligence Summaries are contained in F. S. Regs., Part II. and the Staff Manual respectively. Title pages will be prepared in manuscript.

WAR DIARY
or
INTELLIGENCE SUMMARY.
(Erase heading not required.)

Army Form C. 2118.

Place	Date 1918	Hour	Summary of Events and Information	Remarks and references to Appendices
ELVERDINGHE	Jan 9		attended DDVS Conference at AHQ. Points discussed — Sp Ophthalmia. Foot Cogs. Formation of permanent Corps VCCS personnel to be obtained by taking 1 staff sergt & 6 men from each MVS & an Officer & other ranks equally from hospitals on L of C. Each VCCS to have a personnel of about 40 all told & to do all evacuations & provide train conducting parties. Importance, at the discretion of OC MVS, less than 1 man per truck can be sent to base with sick horses. I consider this an excellent ruling & have often suggested it before as being one way of coping with heavy evacuations & few men.	
	16		attended Conference at AHQ (DDVS) Subjects discussed — Economy in drugs — VCCS. Certain cases of Sp Ophthalmia may be treated in lines at VO's discretion providing they can be segregated.	
	19		Had Conference of VOs at ADVS Office Corps HQ to inform them of subjects raised at DDVS conferences.	

A5834 Wt. W4973/M687 750,000 8/16 D. D. & L. Ltd. Forms/C.2118/13.

138

Army Form C. 2118.

Instructions regarding War Diaries and Intelligence Summaries are contained in F. S. Regs., Part II. and the Staff Manual respectively. Title pages will be prepared in manuscript.

WAR DIARY
~~or~~
~~INTELLIGENCE SUMMARY.~~

(Erase heading not required.)

Place	Date 1918	Hour	Summary of Events and Information	Remarks and references to Appendices
ELVERDINGHE	Jan 22		ADVS XIX Corps returned from leave.	
"	" 27		DADVS on leave to U.K.	
			[illegible] Major DADVS 18 Div	139

A5834 Wt. W4973/M687 750,000 8/16 D. D. & L. Ltd. Forms/C.2118/13.

11

Instructions regarding War Diaries and Intelligence Summaries are contained in F. S. Regs., Part II. and the Staff Manual respectively. Title pages will be prepared in manuscript.

WAR DIARY
~~or~~
~~INTELLIGENCE~~ ~~SUMMARY.~~

(Erase heading not required.)

Army Form C. 2118.

DADVS 18 D

Vol 31

Place	Date 1918	Hour	Summary of Events and Information	Remarks and references to Appendices
			DADVS 18 Div Vol. 32.	
ROUSBRUGGE	Feb 1		DHQ moved to rest area at ROUSBRUGGE rest of the Division in surrounding area	
"	" 7		DHQ moved from ROUSBRUGGE to SALENCY by rail and rest of the Division into surrounding area coming under Fifth Army & III Corps.	
SALENCY	" 9		30 MVS arrived SALENCY.	
	" 11		Acting DADVS went to see ADVS III Corps.	
"	" 12		DADVS returned from leave.	
	" 14		Visited area occupied by 53 Inf Bde Transport arranged for thorough disinfection of all buildings used for stabling & for notices "out of bounds" to be posted on all those not disinfected.	
			Forwarded D.R.O. re disinfecting stables before occupying them in new area taken over from the French.	
			VOs to office	
"	16		30 MVS moved to GRANDRU to start formation of a Corps Collecting Station (to become permanent later)	
BABOEUF	" 17		DHQ moved to BABOEUF.	
	" 18		Met ADVS III Corps at M.V.S.	140

A5834 Wt. W4973 M687 750,000 8/16 D. D. & L. Ltd. Forms/C.2118/13.

Instructions regarding War Diaries and Intelligence Summaries are contained in F. S. Regs., Part II. and the Staff Manual respectively. Title pages will be prepared in manuscript.

WAR DIARY
or
INTELLIGENCE SUMMARY.

(Erase heading not required.)

Army Form C. 2118.

Place	Date 1918	Hour	Summary of Events and Information	Remarks and references to Appendices
BABOEUF	Feb. 21		attended Conference at ADVS Office III Corps. Nothing of importance discussed.	
"	24		Went to GUISCARD and issued 45 Remounts for DAQ [illegible].	
VILLEQUIER-AUMONT	27		DHQ moved to VILLEQUIER-AUMONT to take over portion of line. MVS to remain at GRANDRU by order of III Corps. Capt N. BISSET AVC on leave to ENGLAND.	
	28		Nothing of importance has happened during the month. Condition of all horses generally good & a very great improvement on their condition this time last year. Very little mange or other contagious disease. A good many cases of Ophthalmia which was prevalent in Belgium I should not seem in this part of the country. I do not agree with the various theories lately expounded regarding this disease but consider that it is identical with the sp. of Ophthalmia so common in England before any hygienic conditions were permitted to exist in stables. It has only made its appearance at the front since large concentrations of horse lines have existed & is more prevalent on the fouled soil of Belgium than anywhere else. I have seen no proof of direct contagion.	141

[illegible] Major
DADVS 18 Div

A5834 Wt. W4973/M687 750,000 8/16 D. D. & L. Ltd. Forms/C.2118/13.

27

WAR DIARY
or
INTELLIGENCE SUMMARY.
(*Erase heading not required.*)

Instructions regarding War Diaries and Intelligence Summaries are contained in F. S. Regs., Part II. and the Staff Manual respectively. Title pages will be prepared in manuscript.

Army Form C. 2118.

DADVS 18 D
Vol 32

142

Place	Date 1918	Hour	Summary of Events and Information	Remarks and references to Appendices
			DADVS 18 Div Vol 33 Date of formation of 18 Div Oct 1914. Date of formation of 30 MVS May 1915. Date of proceeding overseas from UK 25.7.15	
VILLEQUIER-AUMONT	Mar. 9.		Visited 79 RE Coy, which has been detached & found an old standing case of Sarcoptic Mange which had not been diagnosed as early as might have been by VO – three others affected also. Gave instructions for the whole unit to be clipped as early as possible.	
	11		ADVS III Corps inspected 82 Bde RFA & considered condition of horses good.	
	12		Evacuated 9 mange cases from 79 RE & some of these animals showed no symptoms until clipped & it is quite likely that more will be diseased as clipping progresses. There is no doubt in my mind that we shall never keep thoroughly free from mange until horses are clipped regularly in spite of all the arguments against clipping during the winter.	
	15		Capt Bird AVC returned from leave to England.	
	16		Attended Conference at ADVS III Corps	
	18		Acting for ADVS III Corps whilst he is at Fifth Army during DDVS on leave. To live with my Division & call daily at Corps Inspected 79 RE where all animals clipped & find 20 more for evac, also 8 cases in 8/Berks which unit is to be clipped out as soon as possible. Arranged with "Q" to send in	

A5834 Wt. W4973/M687 750,000 8/16 D. D. & L. Ltd. Forms/C.2118/13.

Instructions regarding War Diaries and Intelligence Summaries are contained in F. S. Regs., Part II. and the Staff Manual respectively. Title pages will be prepared in manuscript.

WAR DIARY
~~or~~
~~INTELLIGENCE SUMMARY.~~

(Erase heading not required.)

Army Form C. 2118.

Place	Date 1918	Hour	Summary of Events and Information	Remarks and references to Appendices
VILLEQUIER-AUMONT	Mar. 18		an urgent requisition for animals to replace these before they are evacuated as to do so immediately would render the units immobile & this cannot be done in view of a possible enemy offensive shortly.	
..	.. 19		Visited III Corps. H.Q.	
	.. 20		Visited III Corps H.Q.	
..	.. 21		Visited III Corps H.Q. Enemy offensive started 4.30 a.m. by heavy bombardment followed by Infantry attack which carried all front positions on our front capturing all 83 Bde guns & several of 82 Bde. C & D Waggon lines 83 Bde located at MONTESCOURT were heavily shelled, many horses killed & Capt COTTON. AVC lost all his kit, left in wagon lines when the stampede occurred. Rear H.Q. including myself & office moved at midnight to BABOEUF	
BABOEUF	.. 22		Forward D.H.Q. moved to UGNY-le-Gay & III Corps to GUISCARD. Visited D.H.Q. & went to GUISCARD to III Corps, just moving in from UGNY le GAY.	
..	.. 23		Rode to GUISCARD to III Corps HQ & found it just moving out.	
"	.. 24		Visited III Corps H.Q. in NOYON – just moving out again. It is impossible for me to do anything at Corps whilst constantly moving so shall keep with my Division & let the other Divisional ADVS make their own arrangements as we are all constantly moving & the VCCS arrangement did not allow for a continuous & fairly rapid retirement.	143

Instructions regarding War Diaries and Intelligence Summaries are contained in F. S. Regs., Part II. and the Staff Manual respectively. Title pages will be prepared in manuscript.

WAR DIARY
or
~~INTELLIGENCE~~ SUMMARY.

(Erase heading not required.)

Army Form C. 2118.

Place	Date 1918	Hour	Summary of Events and Information	Remarks and references to Appendices
BABIEUF	Mar 24		Had arranged yesterday with RTO APPILLY to evacuate 27 sick horses from there today but on arrival he had just had orders to empty station of all rolling stock so could not take them. Sent them into NOYON & got them on to train there. 1 NCO + 12 [illegible] men arrived from Base & came on with 30 MVS. Marched by P.M. with 30 MVS & 18 Div Train to DIVE-LE-FRANC, [illegible] to THIESCOURT	
DIVE-LE-FRANC	25		Whole of Divisional Transport less RA including MVS & Staff marched to PIMPREZ.	
PIMPREZ	26		Got a chance to put [illegible] men for VCES onto train for Base so returned them as they are not good at marching [illegible]. Marched to CARLEPONT	
CARLEPONT	27		AUDIGNICOURT	
AUDIGNICOURT	28		Joined up with DHQ again who go [illegible] with fighting troops by motor transport to near AMIENS.	
	29		Divisional Transport & 30 MVS marched to CHOISY accompanied 30 MVS in rear of column	
CHOISY	30		ARSY	
ARSY	31		LA NEUVILLE	
			So far casualties which mostly occurred during first few days of the attack = 65 killed and [illegible] 16 destroyed [illegible] 14 missing 27 evacuated. RA suffered more heavily than Infantry owing to Wagon lines being shelled at Commencement. Infantry & ASC are standing the marching well. The places selected for V.C.E.S. had both to be evacuated by the fourth day so it was useless to try & carry it on with formations & railheads constantly moving. Also impossible to collect returns owing to difficulty of communicating with anyone.	144

[illegible signature] Major
DADVS 18 Div.

A5834 Wt. W4973/M687 750,000 8/16 D. D. & L. Ltd. Forms/C.2118/13.

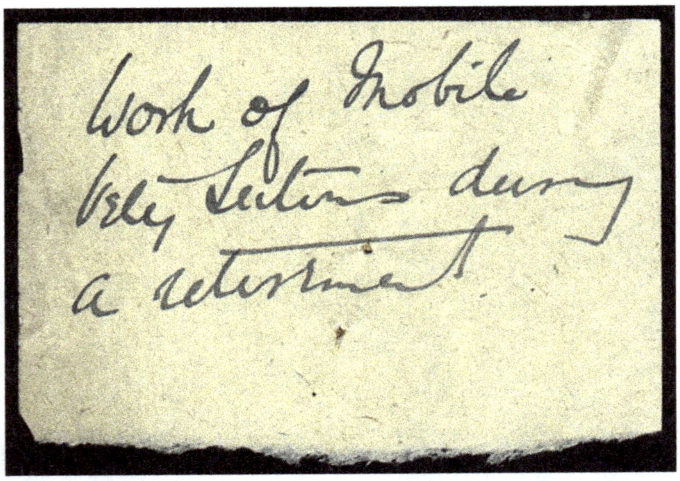

Work of Mobile
Vety Sections during
a retirement.

Instructions regarding War Diaries and Intelligence Summaries are contained in F. S. Regs., Part II. and the Staff Manual respectively. Title pages will be prepared in manuscript.

WAR DIARY ~~or~~ ~~INTELLIGENCE SUMMARY~~.

(Erase heading not required.)

Army Form C. 2118.

~~30 [illegible]~~ DADVS 18 D

33

Place	Date 1918	Hour	Summary of Events and Information	Remarks and references to Appendices
			DADVS. 18 Div. Vol. 34.	
On the march	Apl 1		Marched from LA NEUVILLE to AUCHY-LA-MONTAIGNE	
	" 2		" AUCHY LA MONTAIGNE to LOEUILLY.	
	" 3		LOEUILLY to SALEUX. 18 Div all to POIX neighbourhood to refit.	
SALEUX	" 4		30 MVS located at SALEUX also my office & rear D HQ, Div Train, rear half of Infantry Transports, Fd Ambulances & Sussex Pioneers. Adv HQ at BOVES. Adv Vety Collecting Post established at BOVES with Capt Bissel AVC i/c and also i/c of advanced details of Infantry Transports & RE's	
	" 7		Visited Rear Corps HQ at BOVELLES to see ADVS III Corps & took weekly returns for the last two weeks which it had been impossible to render before owing to constant movement & uncertainty of communication. For the same reason it was impossible for me to carry out the duties of ADVS Corps as well as my own duties as DADVS Div. During a retirement of any length the idea of one Div MVS acting as a VES for the others is not practicable and I doubt whether a permanent VES, under these conditions, would be of any use. It is absolutely essential for the Divl MVS to keep with their own Division &, owing to the constantly changing Railheads it is difficult to carry out the evacuation of sick animals.	145

A5834 Wt. W4973/M687 750,000 8/16 D. D. & L. Ltd. Forms/C.2118/13.

Instructions regarding War Diaries and Intelligence Summaries are contained in F. S. Regs., Part II. and the Staff Manual respectively. Title pages will be prepared in manuscript.

WAR DIARY
~~or~~
INTELLIGENCE SUMMARY.
(*Erase heading not required.*)

Army Form C. 2118.

Place	Date 1918	Hour	Summary of Events and Information	Remarks and references to Appendices
SALEUX	apl. 7		The Mob. Vety Sections of each Division in the Corps managed to evacuate up to nearly the last trains leaving NOYON but this was done individually & not through the Corps and the alternative site for the V.E.S., in the event of a retirement, had to be evacuated very early in the course of operations. Fortunately as regards my own Division there was very little need for evacuation of sick during the march. Whatever the organisation may be the evacuation of sick animals to the Base during a retirement will always be a difficult problem and those that are unable to be taken along with the column will inevitably have to be destroyed.	
	8		ADV Collecting Post at BOVES very congested with wounded animals mostly from other units than 18 Div.	
			Visited 79 RE [illegible] detachment & evacuated 4 mange cases. The rest of this Coy which had mange cases awaiting evacuation has got detached from the Division & cannot be dealt with until it joins up again.	
	13		[illegible] HQ moved from BOVES to St FUSCIEN and ADV C.P. withdrawn from Boves.	
	16		Inspected heavy transports of Fd Coys RE ~~[illegible]~~ on their rejoining the Div & evacuated 5 mange cases from 79 Coy. 18 Div Art arrived at RIVERY. 55 Bde Group moved back to CAVILLON area.	146

A5834 Wt. W4973/M687 750,000 8/16 D. D. & L. Ltd. Forms/C.2118/13.

Mange; and Clipping

Army Form C. 2118.

WAR DIARY
or
INTELLIGENCE SUMMARY.
(Erase heading not required.)

Instructions regarding War Diaries and Intelligence Summaries are contained in F. S. Regs., Part II. and the Staff Manual respectively. Title pages will be prepared in manuscript.

Place	Date 1918	Hour	Summary of Events and Information	Remarks and references to Appendices
SALEUX	Apl. 16.		It is worth noting that the majority of the mange cases in 79 Bde, which could not be evacuated owing to sudden commencement of active operations, instead of getting worse have improved although no treatment other than isolating segregation has been carried out. I attribute this to the fact that the animals were all clipped & picketted in the open during decidedly wintry weather. This has no doubt been a strong factor in inhibiting the powers of propagation of the parasite & tends to prove that clipped animals are much less readily infected with the disease. None of them appear to have lost condition.	
"	" 19		D.V.S. visited No. 30. M.V.S.	
	" 20		Established a Collecting Post at St FUSCIEN.	
	" 24		M.V.S. evacuating a good many debility cases from Army F.A. Bdes in the locality – several destroyed as not worth sending down.	
	" 26		D.H.Q. moved to CAVILLON	
CAVILLON	" 27		My office moved to CAVILLON. M.V.S. remaining at SALEUX to evacuate horses for R.A. & Corps units for a few days. The remainder of Div'l transport moving back into CAVILLON area.	
	" 29		Visited V.E.S. at PICQUIGNY.	
			[illegible] Major D.A.D.V.S. 18 Div	147

A5834 Wt. W4973/M687 750,000 8/16 D. D. & L. Ltd. Forms/C.2118/13.

91

WAR DIARY ~~or~~ INTELLIGENCE SUMMARY.

(*Erase heading not required.*)

Instructions regarding War Diaries and Intelligence Summaries are contained in F. S. Regs., Part II. and the Staff Manual respectively. Title pages will be prepared in manuscript.

Army Form C. 2118.

DADVS 18 Division

Vol 34

Place	Date 1918	Hour	Summary of Events and Information	Remarks and references to Appendices
			~~DADVS 18 Div Vol 35~~	
CAVILLON	May 1		30 MVS arrived 5PM from SALEUX & located at CROUY. Visited by ADVS III Corps.	
	3		Capt ES JELBART medically examined & found to have a hernia so will be evacuated; arranged for Capt COTTON to take temporary duty with 30 MVS.	
	4		Capt COTTON arrived & took over from Capt JELBART.	
	5		Capt JELBART evacuated to No 47 CCS. Am very sorry to lose a most competent officer who has been with me since I joined the 18 Div & is the only original VO, besides myself, left. He has had command of 30 MVS for nearly three years & has always discharged his duties with zeal & efficiency & tact. He will be greatly missed.	
			DHQ moved to BAVLINCOURT	
			30 MVS to MONTIGNY.	
MONTIGNY	6		Moved my office to MONTIGNY & went to live temporarily with 30 MVS owing to no accomodation being available at DHQ.	
	7		Visited III Corps HQ (ADVS out). Evacuations by road to [illegible] VES at OLINCOURT CHATEAU.	148

A5834 Wt. W4973/M687 750,000 8/16 D. D. & L. Ltd. Forms/C.2118/13.

Instructions regarding War Diaries and Intelligence Summaries are contained in F. S. Regs., Part II. and the Staff Manual respectively. Title pages will be prepared in manuscript.

WAR DIARY
or
INTELLIGENCE SUMMARY.
(Erase heading not required.)

Army Form C. 2118.

Place	Date 1918	Hour	Summary of Events and Information	Remarks and references to Appendices
MONTIGNY	May 11		Received instructions from ADVS III Corps to administer 96 AFA Bde	
	" 12		Visited 96 AFA Bde. Horses generally in very poor condition. Wrote report to ADVS III Corps re same.	
	" 14		Weather warm and dry & horses generally looking fairly well with the exception of a few in the RA. Clipping many mules & those animals with thick ragged coats has apparently improved their condition & the only disease which is not decreasing is Sp. Ophthalmia for which no permanent cure has yet been discovered. I still think the cause of this disease is to be found in the occupation of stale standings & the insanitary conditions which are more or less bound to accumulate round standings occupied for any length of time in areas where there is a large concentration of horses. It is impossible to disinfect or purify soil which is constantly soaked with urine & manure & where there is a large concentration of troops it is also impossible to frequently move horselines for new ground especially in districts where there are growing crops. The losses in blind horses from the effects of Sp. Ophthalmia must be getting quite serious but another startling	149

A5834 Wt. W4973 M687 750,000 8/16 D. D. & L. Ltd. Forms/C.2118/13.

Army Form C. 2118.

Instructions regarding War Diaries and Intelligence Summaries are contained in F. S. Regs., Part II. and the Staff Manual respectively. Title pages will be prepared in manuscript.

WAR DIARY
~~or~~
INTELLIGENCE SUMMARY.

(*Erase heading not required.*)

Place	Date 1918	Hour	Summary of Events and Information	Remarks and references to Appendices
MONTIGNY	May 12		conditions I see very little hope for any decrease in this disease	
	" 15		Capt C.E. WOLFE AVC (TC) reported for duty vice Capt IELBART & was posted to 83 Bde RFA.	
	" 17		Surplus men from 30 MVS, on reduction of establishment, despatched to No 7 VES.	
MOLLENS-AU-BOIS	" 25		DHQ moved to MOLLIENS-AU-BOIS & moved my office there. 30 MVS remains at MONTIGNY	
	" 27		Visited III Corps HQ & saw ADVS.	
	" 28		ADVS III Corps visited 30 M.V.S.	
	" 31		Under instructions from O/c AVC Base Records P/A/Staff Sergt WARSOP reduced to sergt & sent to No 2 V.H. being surplus to the establishment & not recommended as a staff sergt for a V.E.S.	

[illegible] Major
DADVS 18 Div

150

A5834 Wt. W4973/M687 750,000 8/16 D. D. & L. Ltd. Forms/C.2118/13.

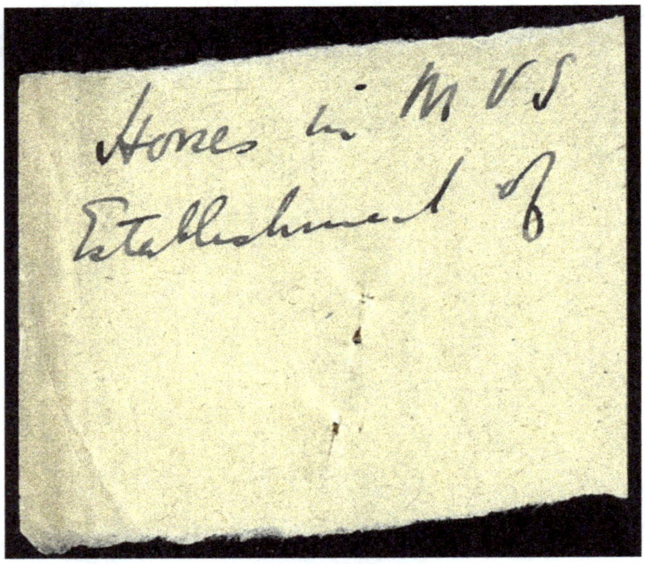

Horses in MVS
Establishment of

Instructions regarding War Diaries and Intelligence Summaries are contained in F. S. Regs., Part II. and the Staff Manual respectively. Title pages will be prepared in manuscript.

27

WAR DIARY
or
INTELLIGENCE SUMMARY.
(Erase heading not required.)

Army Form C. 2118.

DADVS/18D

WO 35

Place	Date 1918	Hour	Summary of Events and Information	Remarks and references to Appendices
			DADVS. 19. Div. Vol. 36.	
MOLLIENS-AU-BOIS	June 2		54 Inf Bde had some bombing casualties & many good horses killed. 55 Bde also lost nine animals from shell fire. Bomb barriers were in course of erection but as the units had only moved to a fresh site the day before they had not had time to complete same.	
	6		Animals are getting a good proportion of green food & generally looking pretty well. There is very little sickness & chief number of evacuations are bomb & shell wounds. The chief cause of worry is Sp Ophthalmia which keeps cropping up & I am afraid the necessity for building bomb barriers round all horse lines will not go towards helping sanitation.	
	14		G.R.O. published again reducing the Riders in an M.V.S. – Total now 11 which means that a certain number of men are permanently dismounted. I do not think this reduction a good thing, especially as now that V.E.S. are established all the evacuations from M.V.S. are done by road & will continue to be so done. This throws a lot of work on the M.V.S. horses when evacuations are large & they are required much more now than	151

A5834 Wt. W4973 M687 750,000 8/16 D. D. & L. Ltd. Forms/C.2118/13.

Instructions regarding War Diaries and Intelligence Summaries are contained in F. S. Regs., Part II. and the Staff Manual respectively. Title pages will be prepared in manuscript.

WAR DIARY
or
~~INTELLIGENCE SUMMARY.~~

(*Erase heading not required.*)

Army Form C. 2118.

Place	Date 1918	Hour	Summary of Events and Information	Remarks and references to Appendices
MOLLIENS AU BOIS	June 14		formerly when a mobile section might have been located near a railhead. There is a very short distance to go. It is stated to be a temporary measure but so was the reduction of ~~the~~ the last V.O., who doesn't appear likely to be replaced.	
	15 to 28		Nothing of special interest to note.	
"	" 29		12 animals killed & 20 wounded by bombing in D/82 wagon line. Good barriers had been erected but unfortunately the bomb fell right inside.	
"	" 30		Remounts are now very short owing to American Divisions having to be horsed from our Depots & this necessitates a falling off in the standard of horses coming up from the Base.	
			[illegible signature] DADVS 18 Div	152

A5834 Wt. W4973/M687 750,000 8/16 D. D. & L. Ltd. Forms/C.2118/13.

27

Instructions regarding War Diaries and Intelligence Summaries are contained in F. S. Regs., Part II. and the Staff Manual respectively. Title pages will be prepared in manuscript.

WAR DIARY

or

INTELLIGENCE SUMMARY.

(Erase heading not required.)

Army Form C. 2118.

DADVS 18 D

98/36

Place	Date 1918	Hour	Summary of Events and Information	Remarks and references to Appendices
			DADVS 18 DIV Vol 34.	
MOLLIENS-AU-BOIS	July 1.		Visited 92 Fd Coy RE & found three thin horses also several thin ones which have not improved as much as they should have done considering the amount of [illegible] green forage available & good weather. Wrote report to CRE recommending more supervision in the horse lines	
	2		Received report from a V.O at No 15 V.H sent through DVS. [illegible] on several horses which he had destroyed on animal on humane grounds & considered that, owing to the serious nature of their injuries, they should not have been despatched to the Base. One of these animals was from my Division & had a large [illegible] wound in the muscles of the quarter. I remember the horse well & purposely kept him in my MVS for five days to see how he progressed. He was doing well & in excellent condition & it was only a question of whether it was worth while giving him the time to recover taking his age into consideration. In any case he would have been an excellent case for the [illegible] & there was no inhumanity whatever in sending him down. I much resent criticism of this kind from the base by people who possibly do not in the least realise the difficulties we have to	153

A5834 Wt. W4973 M687 750,000 8/16 D. D. & L. Ltd. Forms/C.2118/13.

Instructions regarding War Diaries and Intelligence Summaries are contained in F. S. Regs., Part II. and the Staff Manual respectively. Title pages will be prepared in manuscript.

WAR DIARY
or
~~INTELLIGENCE SUMMARY.~~

(Erase heading not required.)

Army Form C. 2118.

Place	Date 1918	Hour	Summary of Events and Information	Remarks and references to Appendices
MOLLIENS-AU-BOIS	July 2		contend with in the forward areas. Destruction is easy & a simple way of disposing of	
			troublesome cases if one has not got the interests of the patient & the State thoroughly at	
			heart. The term "on humane grounds" strikes me as being a peculiarly senseless	
			expression & if it should be justifiable it is very inconsistent to keep the animal	
			alive for another 24 hours to undergo the Mallein Test.	
			Written explaining this particular case & pointed out the fact that the animal	
			had passed through the hands of three Executive and two administrative V.O's	
			before being put on the train & that under these circumstances it was	
			reasonable to question the judgement of the officer at the Base who reported	
			the case as one that should not have been sent down. Apparently this	
			junior officer was able, on his own responsibility, to order the destruction of six	
			or seven animals out of one consignment straight away & the fact that this	
			is possible is not flattering to administrative V.O's of Divisions who make	
			a point of carefully inspecting all patients which pass through their Mobile	
			Vety Sections.	
"	" 4		Capt S.J. COTTON on leave to ENGLAND & Capt J.L. Williams takes temporary charge of 30 M.V.S.	54

A5834 Wt. W4973/M687 750,000 8/16 D. D. & L. Ltd. Forms/C.2118/13.

Instructions regarding War Diaries and Intelligence Summaries are contained in F. S. Regs., Part II. and the Staff Manual respectively. Title pages will be prepared in manuscript.

WAR DIARY
or
INTELLIGENCE SUMMARY.
(*Erase heading not required.*)

Army Form C. 2118.

Place	Date 1918	Hour	Summary of Events and Information	Remarks and references to Appendices
MOLLIENS-AU-BOIS	July 5th		Visited Corps H.Q. at request of A.D.V.S.	
	13		D.H.Q. moved to CAVILLON & 30 M.V.S. to BREILLY (rest area) exchanging with 4? Div.	
CAVILLON	16		D.A.D.V.S. to III Corps H.Q. to officiate for A.D.V.S. whilst on leave.	
			Capt J.L. WILLIAMS to D.H.Q. to officiate for D.A.D.V.S.	
			Weather good, animals generally looking well & very little sickness or wastage.	
	22		Capt S.J. COTTON returned from leave to Nº 30 M.V.S.	
	28		Wrote in through A.D.V.S. & D.D.V.S. asking for Capt S.E. JELBART to be re-posted to 30 M.V.S. on recovery.	
	30		D.A.D.V.S. returned to D.H.Q. from Corps H.Q. & Capt J.L. Williams rejoined 82 Bde R.F.A.	
	31		30 M.V.S. moved to St GRATIEN wood & took over lines occupied by 5th Aust Div Mob. Vet Section.	
			Hay Ration for horses still further reduced so that H.D. horses only get 11 lbs. This is not enough & will be sure to affect their condition if continued for long.	
			[illegible] Major D.A.D.V.S. 18 Div	155

A5834 Wt. W4973/M687 750,000 8/16 D. D. & L. Ltd. Forms/C.2118/13.

27

Instructions regarding War Diaries and Intelligence Summaries are contained in F. S. Regs., Part II. and the Staff Manual respectively. Title pages will be prepared in manuscript.

WAR DIARY
or
INTELLIGENCE SUMMARY.
(Erase heading not required.)

Army Form C. 2118.

DADVS 18 D

V 37

Place	Date 1918	Hour	Summary of Events and Information	Remarks and references to Appendices
			DADVS 18th Div Vol No. 38.	
St GRATIEN	Aug 1.		DHQ moved from CAVILLON to ST GRATIEN in relief of 5th Aust Div.	
..	.. 6		Visited neighbourhood of HEILLY with OC MVS to pick site for an adv vety aid post when offensive operations commence.	
	.. 7		Established adv vety post at J 7 A (6 2 8)	
	.. 8		Offensive operations commenced on Div front. Received telegram through DHQ saying Capt JELBART shortly arriving from England & re posted to 30 MVS for duty.	
	10		Capt J.L. Williams on leave to ENGLAND till 24.8.18.	
	11		Adv Vety Post withdrawn. Casualties fortunately very light so far.	
CONTAY	.. 12		DHQ moved to CONTAY. 30 MVS to MONTIGNY (B24 c 2.4)	
..	.. 15		Capt E.E. JELBART arrived from England & resumed command of 30 MVS.	
..	.. 17		Capt S.J. COTTON evacuated to CCS with Sciatica.	
..	21		Established adv vety post at WARLOY (U23 D 9.7)	
	24		30 MVS moved to WARLOY.	
WARLOY	25		DHQ moved to WARLOY & HENENCOURT CHATEAU.	156

A5834 Wt. W4973 M687 750,000 8/16 D. D. & L. Ltd. Forms/C.2118/13.

Instructions regarding War Diaries and Intelligence Summaries are contained in F. S. Regs., Part II. and the Staff Manual respectively. Title pages will be prepared in manuscript.

WAR DIARY
or
INTELLIGENCE SUMMARY.
(Erase heading not required.)

Army Form C. 2118.

Place	Date 1918	Hour	Summary of Events and Information	Remarks and references to Appendices
WARLOY	Augst 26		30 M.V.S. moved to BELLEVUE FARM.	
			Capt J.L. Williams reported his arrival from leave.	
HENENCOURT	" 28		Moved my office to Henencourt Chateau	
	" 29		Visited WARLOY to see 6 D.G.s Evacuated 16 wounded horses to No 3 V.E.S.	
	" 31		Adv HQ moved to TRONES WOOD & A+Q to BECOURT CHATEAU.	
			my office remaining here at present.	
			On leaving the R. Ancre water will be a difficult problem as we shall be entirely dependent on wells which are very deep before the water level is reached.	
			[signature] Major ADVS 18 DW.	

157

A5834 Wt. W4973/M687 750,000 8/16 D. D. & L. Ltd. Forms/C.2118/13.

Instructions regarding War Diaries and Intelligence Summaries are contained in F. S. Regs., Part II. and the Staff Manual respectively. Title pages will be prepared in manuscript.

WAR DIARY
~~or~~
~~INTELLIGENCE~~ SUMMARY.
(Erase heading not required.)

Army Form C. 2118.

DADVS 18 Div

Vol 39

Place	Date 1918	Hour	Summary of Events and Information	Remarks and references to Appendices
			DADVS 18 Div Vol No 39	
HENENCOURT Chateau	Sept. 2		Moved to Caterpillar Wood S20 d2.4	
Caterpillar Wood	" 7		Very little sickness & although food ration reduced from normal quantity horses are looking very well generally owing to plenty of rough grazing being available in the vicinity of most transport & wagon lines. Water has been the chief trouble during the last week but the supply is improving.	
"	" 8		DDVS & ADVS visited 30 MVS. 83 Bde RFA came back from forward area for a few days rest.	
"	" 10		~~Corps Commander~~ Accompanied Corps Commander on his inspection of the horses of 83 Bde. He expressed his satisfaction ~~at the~~ with the general condition of the horses considering the work they have been doing since the commencement of active operations.	
"	" 11		83 Bde & No 2 Sec DAC went back to forward area.	
"	" 15		Attended Plateau Railhead to issue 133 Remounts for DA & Bdes due to arrive 12 noon & waited until 6 am on 16th when the train came in, a fairly good sample taken altogether.	158

Instructions regarding War Diaries and Intelligence Summaries are contained in F. S. Regs., Part II. and the Staff Manual respectively. Title pages will be prepared in manuscript.

WAR DIARY
~~or~~
~~INTELLIGENCE SUMMARY.~~
(*Erase heading not required.*)

Army Form C. 2118.

Place	Date 1918	Hour	Summary of Events and Information	Remarks and references to Appendices
Caterpillar Wood	Sept. 18		DADOS proceeded on special leave to England. Capt E.E. Gelbart officiating.	
			DHQ & office of DADOS moved to Trucker Wood.	
Trucker Wood	" 25		moved to COMBLES.	
COMBLES	" 28		Inspected horses of 83 Bde RFA which have lost considerably in condition during the last three weeks & are feeling the effects of shortage of forage now that grazing is not so plentiful & the result of being on reduced forage ration is that, even when on full rations the daily allowance is frequently not up to full scale, & the same thing happens when on a reduced ration when it is much more seriously felt. I fear that unless it is possible to issue a larger daily ration very soon we shall lose a lot of animals from Debility during the winter. This is the worst time of the year for horses to be losing condition as they do not get a fair start before the bad weather & can rarely make it up again.	

E.M. [illegible] Major
DADOS 18 Div

159

A5834 Wt. W4973/M687 750,000 8/16 D. D. & L. Ltd. Forms/C.2118/13.

9

Instructions regarding War Diaries and Intelligence Summaries are contained in F. S. Regs., Part II, and the Staff Manual respectively. Title pages will be prepared in manuscript.

WAR DIARY
or
INTELLIGENCE SUMMARY.
(Erase heading not required.)

Army Form C. 2118.

DADVS 18 D

18 40

Place	Date	Hour	Summary of Events and Information	Remarks and references to Appendices
			DADVS 18 Div Vol No. 40. Sh 1.	
BEAUCOURT Sur L'HALLUE	4 10/18		Major L.M. Verney A.V.C. rejoined from leave to England	
			Capt N. Bisset granted leave to U K 4 to 18 10/18	
	5 10/18		Inspected Sussex Pioneer animals, 55 Field Ambulance and 7th Buffs	
	6 10/18		" 153 Co ASC 18 M G Battn + 92 Fd Co R.E.	
	7 10/18		Visited D.D.V.S. Fourth Army when he informed Major Verney it was proposed to post him temporarily to II American Corps as ADVS.	
	8 10/18		Visited 55 Fd Ambulance 153 Co ASC 55 Bde HQ + 92 Fd Co R.E.	
	9 10/18		" 79 Fd Co RE 7th Queens 8 E. Surreys 80 Fd Co R.E., M.V.S. + signals	
	10 10/18		Visited 18 M.G Battn + 153 Co A.S.C.	
	11 10/18		Major L M VERNEY A.V.C. left for temporary duty with II American Corps Authy QMG wire Q.P. 2555 of 5.X.18. Capt F.F. JELBART A.V.C. instructed to officiate as D.A.D.V.S until Major Verney returns. Authy DDVS Fourth Army P 104/18 d. 10.X.18	
	16 10/18		Report received from U. K. that Capt Bisset – on leave – sick & unable to travel – probably for 14 days.	

A5834 Wt. W4973/M687 750,000 8/16 D. D. & L. Ltd. Forms/C.2118/13.

Instructions regarding War Diaries and Intelligence Summaries are contained in F. S. Regs., Part II. and the Staff Manual respectively. Title pages will be prepared in manuscript.

WAR DIARY
or
INTELLIGENCE SUMMARY.
(Erase heading not required.)

Army Form C. 2118.

Place	Date	Hour	Summary of Events and Information	Remarks and references to Appendices
			(D.A.D.V.S. 18 Div. Vol 40 Sh. 2.)	
BEAUCOURT SUR L'HALLUE	16.10.18		Since arriving in this area the animals of the Div. (except R.A. which are left in the fighting line) have benefitted considerably by the advantage taken of grazing & the rest it has been able to give them	
RONSSOY WOOD	17.10.18		Moved with Div. H.Q. to Ronssoy Wood Sh. 62 C F21 a.	
SERAIN	19.10.18		" " " to SERAIN. Sh. 57B V 14	
MARETZ	20.10.18		" " " " MARETZ Sh. 57B V 6.	
			" " " " " Division rejoined by its artillery	
LE CATEAU	24.10.18		Moved with Div. HQ to LE CATEAU	
	27.10.18		Inspected animals of No 2 Sect 18 DAC	
	28.10.18		Inspected animals of A B & D Btys 83 Bde	
			Since arrival in MARETZ M.V.S. have been busy evacuating considerable numbers of animals mostly of other formations and mostly gunshot casualties. During the week ending 31.10.18 there were 96 casualties to animals of the Division from enemy shell fire 46 killed & 50 wounded. These were mostly due to an enemy long range battery.	
			30 M.V.S. have recently got a new Horse ambulance. The pattern is most unsuitable for the work required of it – as it is excessively heavy – & has very little clearance over the road. A lighter cart & built not so low would last longer & be more useful.	161

[illegible] Capt AVC a/DADVS 18 Div.

A5834 Wt. W4973 M687 750,000 8/16 D. D. & L. Ltd. Forms/C.2118/13.

Instructions regarding War Diaries and Intelligence Summaries are contained in F. S. Regs., Part II. and the Staff Manual respectively. Title pages will be prepared in manuscript.

7/2

WAR DIARY
or
INTELLIGENCE SUMMARY.
(Erase heading not required.)

Army Form C. 2118.

DADVS 18 D

Vol 41

Place	Date	Hour	Summary of Events and Information	Remarks and references to Appendices
	1918		DADVS 18 Div Vol No 41	
LE CATEAU	Nov 2		Capt J. BUIE AVC (TC) reported for duty vice Capt N. BISSET sick in England. Posted to 30 MVS for temporary duty as O.C.	
	5		Very little sickness amongst animals chief cause of casualties being due to active operations. Condition fairly good considering amount of work being done & scale of forage ration. Coats naturally looking rough & dirty.	
	11		Armistice day.	
SERAIN	13		DHQ moved to SERAIN also No 30 MVS	
	14		Visited No 13 VES at HONNECHY & also Army Head Quarters located at same place	
	15		Most of the transport animals are under cover in this area & not working very hard so should improve in condition.	162

A5834 Wt. W4973/M687 750,000 8/16 D. D. & L. Ltd. Forms/C.2118/13.

Instructions regarding War Diaries and Intelligence Summaries are contained in F. S. Regs., Part II. and the Staff Manual respectively. Title pages will be prepared in manuscript.

WAR DIARY
~~or~~
INTELLIGENCE SUMMARY.
(Erase heading not required.)

Army Form C. 2118.

Place	Date 1918	Hour	Summary of Events and Information	Remarks and references to Appendices
SERAIN	Nov 25		Major L. M. VERNEY AVC, DADVS returned from temporary duty as DADVS II Army Corps. Capt JELBART resumed command of No. 30 MVS and Capt BUIE was posted to 18 Div Train. This makes the Division now complete in its establishment of Veterinary Officers.	

L M Verney Major
DADVS 18 Div

163

A5834 Wt. W4973/M687 750,000 8/16 D. D. & L. Ltd. Forms/C.2118/13.

164

18DW. A. 19/2

Herewith War Diary for Dec 1918
Please acknowledge receipt hereon.

2/1/19

[illegible] Major
[illegible]

Instructions regarding War Diaries and Intelligence Summaries are contained in F. S. Regs., Part II. and the Staff Manual respectively. Title pages will be prepared in manuscript.

WAR DIARY
~~or~~
~~INTELLIGENCE~~ SUMMARY.
(*Erase heading not required.*)

Army Form C. 2118.

DADVS 18 D

V8 4 3

Place	Date 1918	Hour	Summary of Events and Information	Remarks and references to Appendices
			DADVS 18 Div Vol No. 42.	
SERAIN	Dec. 14		ADVS XIII Corps inspected horses of 82 Bde RFA & found their condition to be satisfactory.	
LIGNY	" 17		DHQ & my office moved to LIGNY-en-Cambresis. also 30. M.V.S.	
"	" 21		ADVS XIII Corps inspected ~~the~~ animals of 18 D.A.C. & found their condition satisfactory.	
~~LIG~~ "	" 22		attended inspection of mares by Corps Committee at ELINCOURT to pick out likely animals to brand for breeding purposes. Only one mare likely to breed ponies was branded to show to B of A later.	
"	" 29		In accordance with instructions received from D.V.S. a Vety Board of Officers commenced the classification of animals according to age & soundness for purposes of demobilization. Board composed of DADVS, OC MVS & VO of the unit. One battery (A/82) examined & classified.	
"	30		Vety Board classifying animals all day.	

A5834 Wt. W4973/M687 750,000 8/16 D. D. & L. Ltd. Forms/C.2118/13.

165

Army Form C. 2118.

WAR DIARY

or

INTELLIGENCE SUMMARY.

(Erase heading not required.)

Instructions regarding War Diaries and Intelligence Summaries are contained in F. S. Regs., Part II. and the Staff Manual respectively. Title pages will be prepared in manuscript.

Place	Date 1918	Hour	Summary of Events and Information	Remarks and references to Appendices
LIGNY	Dec 31		Vety Board classifying animals all day. Chief cause of uselessness found to be blindness & partial blindness as the result of recurrent attacks of Sp. Ophthalmia, showing the progressive nature of this disease which appears to nearly always terminate in causing complete blindness. Many of these blind draught animals will be fit to do steady work.	

[illegible] Maj.
[illegible]

A5834 Wt. W4973/M687 750,000 8/16 D. D. & L. Ltd. Forms/C.2118/13.

31

Instructions regarding War Diaries and Intelligence Summaries are contained in F. S. Regs., Part II. and the Staff Manual respectively. Title pages will be prepared in manuscript.

WAR DIARY
~~or~~
INTELLIGENCE SUMMARY.
(Erase heading not required.)

Army Form C. 2118.

18 Divn

Vol 44

Place	Date 1919	Hour	Summary of Events and Information	Remarks and references to Appendices
			DADVS 18 Div. Vol. 43.	
LIGNY	Jan. 1		Vety Board examining & classifying horses of RA.	
"	" 2		Visited ADVS XIII Corps & had consultation re classification of horses for Demobilisation	
"	" 3		Vety Board classifying RA. animals.	
"	" 4		Vety Board classifying RA & ASC animals.	
"	" 5		Vety Board classifying RE animals.	
"	" 6		Vety Board " " RA	
"	" 7		Vety Board " " RA. RE & ASC animals.	
"	" 8		Vety Board " " RA. Infantry & M.G. Batt animals.	
"	" 9		Vety Board " " M.G. Batt, Infantry, & RAMC "	
"	" 10		Vety Board " " Infantry Transports & RE.	
"	" 12		Vety Board " " DAC & ASC animals.	
"	" 13		Vety Board " " DAC & Infantry Transports.	
"	" 14		Vety Board " " Infantry Transports.	166

D. D. & L., London, E.C. (A10266) Wt W5300/P713 750,000 2/18 Sch. 52 Forms/C2118/16

Instructions regarding War Diaries and Intelligence Summaries are contained in F. S. Regs., Part II. and the Staff Manual respectively. Title pages will be prepared in manuscript.

WAR DIARY
~~or~~
INTELLIGENCE ~~SUMMARY~~.
(Erase heading not required.)

Army Form C. 2118.

Place	Date 1919	Hour	Summary of Events and Information	Remarks and references to Appendices
LIGNY	Jan 15		Veterinary classification of animals of 18 Div now completed & return forwarded to ~~ADVS~~ XIII Corps as under.	
			Group A. Horses 695 Mules 586	
			" B " 725 " 229	
			" C – " 437 " 127	
			" C2 " 649 " 227	
			" D " 19 " 4	
			Orders now received to Mallein Test all animals which are not for retention in the Army.	
	" [illegible]		Indented urgently for Syringes & mallein. ~~[illegible]~~	
	" 17		Mallein arrived but telegram from No. 1 A Depot Vety Stores saying no syringes available which is extremely inconvenient as I have only two syringes & two needles – sent one of these to VO i/c 82 Bde to carry on with his work.	
	" 20		~~[illegible]~~ Malleining RE & Infantry Transports.	
	" 21		Malleining Infantry Transport & ASC Two new syringes arrived by post.	167

D. D. & L., London, E.C.
(A10266) Wt W5300/P713 750,000 2/18 Sch. 52 Forms/C2118/16

Instructions regarding War Diaries and Intelligence Summaries are contained in F. S. Regs., Part II. and the Staff Manual respectively. Title pages will be prepared in manuscript.

WAR DIARY
or
INTELLIGENCE SUMMARY.
(Erase heading not required.)

Army Form C. 2118.

Place	Date 1919	Hour	Summary of Events and Information	Remarks and references to Appendices
LIGNY	Jan 22		Malleining Infantry Transport, RASC, RE. Capt E.E. JELBART proceeded on leave to ENGLAND & Capt BUIE took over temporarily 30 MVS.	
	23		Malleining Infantry Transport, RAMC, Mg Batt & ASC. D.W. Artillery animals mallein testing completed.	
	24		Visited REUMONT & MARETZ & inspected 200 Y animals to be despatched tomorrow to go to ENGLAND. Malleining 30 MVS & Signals.	
	25		Mallein testing RAMC & 79 RE	
	26		Mallein testing DHQ & other odd animals to finish up. Practically all the Y & Z animals of the Division have now been mallein tested & the whole of this month has been very strenuous for the Vety Service as the area is very wide necessitating long journeys every day & practically all day out both for classification & mallein testing.	
	27		Visited MARETZ & inspected 62 animals of 84 AFA Bde before proceeding to Collecting Camp for sale to Belgians.	168

D. D. & L., London, E.C.
(A10266) Wt W5300/P713 750,000 2/18 Sch. 52 Forms/C2118/16

Army Form C. 2118.

Instructions regarding War Diaries and Intelligence Summaries are contained in F. S. Regs., Part II. and the Staff Manual respectively. Title pages will be prepared in manuscript.

WAR DIARY

~~or~~

~~INTELLIGENCE~~ SUMMARY.

(*Erase heading not required.*)

Place	Date	Hour	Summary of Events and Information	Remarks and references to Appendices
	1919			
LIGNY	Jan. 28		DADVS to this Corps as A/ADVS during absence of ADVS on leave. Capt. J. BUIE officiates for DADVS.	

[illegible] Major
DADVS 28 Div

169

D. D. & L., London, E.C.
(A10266) Wt W5300/P713 750,000 2/18 Sch. 52 Forms/C2118/16

Instructions regarding War Diaries and Intelligence Summaries are contained in F. S. Regs., Part II. and the Staff Manual respectively. Title pages will be prepared in manuscript.

WAR DIARY
or
INTELLIGENCE SUMMARY.
(Erase heading not required.)

Army Form C. 2118.

Place	Date	Hour	Summary of Events and Information	Remarks and references to Appendices
	1919		[illegible] Vol 44	
LIGNY	Feb 1		145 Y animals inspected before despatch to Base.	
	3		34 Y HD animals inspected before despatch to Base.	
	5		78 HD Y animals inspected before despatch to Base.	
			Capt E.E. JELBART returns from leave to England.	
	7		10 CZ animals selected for sale	
	8		9 CZ animals selected for sale	
			Capt J.E. WILLIAMS RAVC to CCS with Influenza	
	10		Inspecting Healthy CZ animals for sale.	
	13		100 CZ animals sold by Auction at MARETZ average price 71½ fr.	
			30 MVS moved to CAMBRAI by orders of DDVS 3rd Army	
	14		[illegible] returns from [illegible]	
	15		Attended sales at SOLESMES & LE CATEAU	
	17		Visited 30 MVS at CAMBRAI	170

D. D. & L., London, E.C.
(A10266) Wt W5300/P713 750,000 2/18 Sch. 52 Forms/C2118/16

Instructions regarding War Diaries and Intelligence Summaries are contained in F. S. Regs., Part II. and the Staff Manual respectively. Title pages will be prepared in manuscript.

WAR DIARY
or
~~INTELLIGENCE SUMMARY.~~
(Erase heading not required.)

Army Form C. 2118.

Place	Date	Hour	Summary of Events and Information	Remarks and references to Appendices
	1919			
LIGNY	Feb. 18		Selecting CZ animals for sale ~~tue~~ on Thursday.	
	19		Selecting CZ animals for sale on Saturday.	
	20		Attended sale of 100 CZ animals at WALINCOURT average price 775 frs	
			Received warning order to go to XV Corps as ADVS	
	22		Attended sale of 100 CZ animals at MARETZ	
	23		Inspecting 1C animals with DADR	
	24		Major G WILLIAMSON arrived to assume duty as DADVS 17 Div	
			Attended sale at WALINCOURT with Major Williamson	
	27		Inspecting CZ animals for despatch to ABBEVILLE & also for sale	
	28		Major G WILLIAMSON assumes duty as DADVS 17 Div Transferred from Major L M VERNEY who is posted to XV Corps as ADVS	
			Williamson Major DADVS 17 Div	

D. D. & L., London, E.C.
(A10266) Wt W5300/P713 750,000 2/18 Sch. 52 Forms/C2118/16

Instructions regarding War Diaries and Intelligence Summaries are contained in F. S. Regs., Part II. and the Staff Manual respectively. Title pages will be prepared in manuscript.

WAR DIARY
or
INTELLIGENCE SUMMARY.
(Erase heading not required.)

Army Form C. 2118.

DADVS 18 D

Vol 45

Place	Date	Hour	Summary of Events and Information	Remarks and references to Appendices
			(DADVS 18th Div Vol 45) Ch 1	
[illegible]IGNY	1-3-19		Took over duties from MAJOR VERNEY. Inspected M.V.S. [illegible] CAMBRAI	
			Sale of 102 Z animals at WALLINCOURT. Average price obtained was 374 francs. Only 65 horses & 27 Mules were sold	
	2-3-19		Inspected 125 Z animals being despatched to ABBEVILLE – [illegible] from Artillery 24 from Trains	[illegible]
	3-3-19		" all Z animals ~~[illegible]~~ with D.A.D.R. for reclassification – 52nd Inf Bde, all Fld Ambulances, R.E. Coys & Machine Gun Battn	[illegible]
	4-3-19		Inspected animals of Train for reclassification	[illegible]
	5-3-19		The M.V.S. was sent to CAMBRAI to form a Receiving Station and to [illegible] 'D' animals from there to CAUDRY. Since the 15th of last month 152 of these have passed through and only 20 animals have been admitted for treatment. Practically all [illegible] [illegible] [illegible] the [illegible]. Class D animals have for the present at least ceased going through [illegible] so that the work of the M.V.S. has practically all ceased. The A.D.V.S. has therefore been requested to allow the Section to come back to the Divisional Area	[illegible]
	6-3-19		Sale of 170 Z animals at ELINCOURT. 93 [illegible] [illegible] were disposed of at a price very little greater than Butcher's price. The average horse price [illegible] [illegible] sold very good	
	7-3-19		Inspected and [illegible] 35 animals for sale at LIGNY [illegible]	172

D. D. & L., London, E.C.
(A10266) Wt W5300/P713 750,000 2/18 Sch. 52 Forms/C2118/16

Army Form C. 2118.

Instructions regarding War Diaries and Intelligence Summaries are contained in F. S. Regs., Part II. and the Staff Manual respectively. Title pages will be prepared in manuscript.

WAR DIARY
or
INTELLIGENCE SUMMARY.

(Erase heading not required.)

Place	Date	Hour	Summary of Events and Information (DADVS 18th Div Vol 46) [illegible]	Remarks and references to Appendices
[illegible]IGNY	8.3.19		[illegible] 43 horses 49 mules [illegible] 200 Z [illegible] ABBEVILLE [illegible]	
	9.3.19		[illegible] CAMBRAI [illegible] HVS [illegible] 30 [illegible]	[illegible]
	10.3.19		[illegible]	
	11.3.19		[illegible] 38 X [illegible] 7 Y [illegible] UK. [illegible] X [illegible] ADVS Corps	[illegible]
	12.3.19		[illegible] 100 [illegible] 13th [illegible] BEAUVOIS [illegible]	[illegible]
	13.3.19		50 X	[illegible]
	14.3.19		Sold at CAMBRAI 50 horses 36 mules [illegible] 463 [illegible] 16 [illegible] 100 Z [illegible] LIGNY.	[illegible]
	15.3.19		45 horses 56 mules [illegible] 500 [illegible]	
	16.3.19		[illegible] CAMBRAI [illegible] 11th 105 [illegible]	
	17.3.19		[illegible]	
	18.3.19		41 horses 24 mules [illegible] CAMBRAI [illegible] 682 [illegible]	[illegible]

173

D. D. & L., London, E.C.
(A10266) Wt W5300/P713 750,000 2/18 Sch. 52 Forms/C2118/16

Instructions regarding War Diaries and Intelligence Summaries are contained in F. S. Regs., Part II. and the Staff Manual respectively. Title pages will be prepared in manuscript.

WAR DIARY
or
INTELLIGENCE SUMMARY.
(Erase heading not required.)

Army Form C. 2118.

Place	Date	Hour	(DADVS 18th Div. Vol 45) Vol 3. Summary of Events and Information	Remarks and references to Appendices
[illegible]GNY			Mules sold well	
			Inspected 50 Z animals entrained for ABBEVILLE	
			50 Y leaving [illegible]	
		14-3-19	As practically all animals are now [illegible] A [illegible] all V.Os & RAVC [illegible] surplus to requirements, except those with the MVS ADVS & Records informed	[illegible]
			Inspected 50 X animals leaving for DIEPPE	
			50 Z ABBEVILLE	[illegible]
		20-3-19	350 X for 2nd Army [illegible]	
			[illegible]	[illegible]
		21-3-19	Inspected [illegible] 28 animals for [illegible] No [illegible] MVS returned from CAMBRAI	[illegible]
		22-3-19	[illegible] 26 horses 2 mules [illegible] 7/6 [illegible]	[illegible]
			[illegible]	
		25-3-19	[illegible] RAVC [illegible]	[illegible]
		26-3-19	Routine work	[illegible]
		27-3-19	"	[illegible]
		28-3-19	Inspected 50 Y animals & 7 Y [illegible]	[illegible]
		29-3-19	Routine Work	[illegible]
		30-3-19	Inspected 25 Y animals [illegible]	
		31-3-19	All [illegible]	[illegible]
		[illegible]-3-19	Routine work	

174

D. D. & L., London, E.C.
(A10266) Wt W5300/P713 750,000 2/18 Sch. 52 Forms/C2118/16

Army Form C. 2118.

Instructions regarding War Diaries and Intelligence Summaries are contained in F. S. Regs., Part II. and the Staff Manual respectively. Title pages will be prepared in manuscript.

WAR DIARY

or

INTELLIGENCE ~~SUMMARY~~.

(Erase heading not required.)

Place	Date	Hour	Summary of Events and Information	Remarks and references to Appendices
			(DADVS 18th Div Vol 45) Sh 2	
16 N.Y	31.3.19		[illegible] CAMBRAI [illegible] 242 [illegible] 439.5 [illegible] 319 [illegible] 787 [illegible]	
			[illegible] 21437 Kgs of oats and 16872 Kgs [illegible]	
			[illegible]	
			All V.Os except myself are under orders to leave the Division [illegible]	
			[illegible]	[illegible]
			C.H. Williamson Maj. RAVC	

175

D. D. & L., London, E.C.
(A10266) Wt W5300/P713 750,000 2/15 Sch. 52 Forms/C2118/16

Instructions regarding War Diaries and Intelligence Summaries are contained in F. S. Regs., Part II. and the Staff Manual respectively. Title pages will be prepared in manuscript.

WAR DIARY
or
INTELLIGENCE SUMMARY.
(*Erase heading not required.*)

Army Form C. 2118.

Place	Date	Hour	Summary of Events and Information	Remarks and references to Appendices
			DADVS 18 DIV Vol 45. Sh 1	
LIGNY	1-3-19		Took over duties from MAJOR VERNEY. Inspected M.V.S at CAMBRAI.	
			Sale of 100 Z animals at WALLINCOURT. Average price obtained was 574 francs. Only 48 horses & 27 mules were sold	
	2-3-19		Inspected 125 Z animals being despatched to ABBEVILLE – 100 from Artillery 25 from Pioneers	[initials]
	3-3-19		" all Z animals ~~[illegible]~~ with D.A.D.R. for reclassification in 52nd Inf Bde. All Fld Ambulances, R.E. Coys & Machine Gun Battn.	[initials]
	4-3-19		Inspected animals of Train for reclassification	[initials]
	5-3-19		The MVS was sent to CAMBRAI to form a Receiving Station and to conduct "D" animals from there to CAUDRY. Since the 15th of last month 152 of these have passed through and only 20 cases have been admitted for treatment. Practically all were chronic cases and were sent to the butcher. Class "D" animals have for the present at least stopped coming through Cambrai so that the work of the M.V.S. has practically ceased. The ADVS has therefore been requested to allow the Section to return to the Divisional area	[initials]
	6-3-19		Sale of 100 Z animals at ELINCOURT. 43 large mules were disposed of at a price very little greater than "butcher price". The average horse price considering the class of animal sold was good	
	7-3-19		Inspected and arranged 85 animals for sale at LIGNY tomorrow	[initials]

176

D. D. & L., London, E.C.
(A10266) Wt W5300/P713 750,000 2/18 Sch. 52 Forms/C2118/16

Instructions regarding War Diaries and Intelligence Summaries are contained in F. S. Regs., Part II. and the Staff Manual respectively. Title pages will be prepared in manuscript.

~~WAR DIARY~~ or INTELLIGENCE SUMMARY.

(Erase heading not required.)

Army Form C. 2118.

177

Place	Date	Hour	(2 A.A.V.S. 18th Div Vol 45) 2	Remarks and references to Appendices
LIGNY	8-3-19		Sold ~~here~~ 43 horses 49 mules. Inspected 200 "Z" horses proceeding to ABBEVILLE 10th inst.	
	9-3-19		As other Division's sales have stopped at CAMBRAI two for this Division were arranged there. Instructed M.V.S. to sell 30 "Z" animals there as there is no demand for them here.	[illegible]
	10-3-19		Routine work.	
	11-3-19		Inspected 58 X horses & 7 Y horses from various units proceeding to U.K. The fact that the "X" animals had not been mallein'd was reported to A.D.V.S. Corps.	[illegible]
	12-3-19		Inspected and prepared 100 horses and mules from Artillery for sale of 13th inst. " 50 "Y" horses proceeding to BEAUVOIS	[illegible]
	13-3-19		" 50 "X" " "	[illegible]
	14-3-19		Sold at CAMBRAI 50 horses 36 mules. Average price 463 francs. The privilege allowed of buying 14 days ration was taken advantage of ~~[illegible]~~ by most buyers and perhaps accounted for the rise in the average price obtained. Mules continue to sell badly. Inspected and prepared 100 Z animals for sale tomorrow at LIGNY.	[illegible]
	15-3-19		45 horses 58 mules sold here. Average price 500 frcs. Forage was again distributed.	
	16-3-19		Inspected and arranged for sale at CAMBRAI on 18th. 186 animals.	
	17-3-19		Routine Work.	
	18-3-19		91 horses 24 mules sold at CAMBRAI. Average price 652 frcs. The horses were mostly bad class of riders and pack ponies. The latter commanded a fair price but the former were hard to sell.	[illegible]

D. D. & L., London, E.C.
(A10266) Wt W5300/P713 750,000 2/18 Sch. 52 Forms/C2118/16

Army Form C. 2118.

Instructions regarding War Diaries and Intelligence Summaries are contained in F. S. Regs., Part II. and the Staff Manual respectively. Title pages will be prepared in manuscript.

WAR DIARY
or
INTELLIGENCE SUMMARY.
(Erase heading not required.)

178

Place	Date	Hour	(D.A.D.V.S. 18th Div Vol 45) Vol 3 — Summary of Events and Information	Remarks and references to Appendices
LIGNY.			Mules sold well	
			Inspected 50 Z animals entrained for ABBEVILLE	
			50 X " leaving the Division	
		19-3-19	As practically all units are now down to "A" Cadre all V.O.s & R.A.V.C. Sergts are surplus to requirements, except those in the M.V.S., A.D.V.S. & Records informed	
			Inspected 50 X animals leaving for DIEPPE	
			" 50 Z " ABBEVILLE	
		20-3-19	350 X for 2nd Army The rider class appeared to be poor and the mules were not of the best	
		21-3-19	Inspected & prepared 28 animals for sale [illegible]. No 3[illegible] M.V.S. returned from CAMBRAI.	
		22-3-19	Local sale 26 horses 2 mules average price 716 frs. This was very high considering the class of animal — cobs & bad class of rider	
		23-3-19	All releasable R.A.V.C. Sergts ordered to No 2 Vety Hosp for demobilization	
		24-3-19	Routine work	
		25-3-19	" "	
		26-3-19	Inspected 50 X animals & 4 Y [illegible] for Base	
		27-3-19	Routine Work	
		28-3-19	Inspected 28 X animals leaving for Base	
		29-3-19	All Vety Sergts attached to units have now been withdrawn	
		30-3-19	Routine work	

D. D. & L., London, E.C.
(A10266) Wt W5300/P713 750,000 2/18 Sch. 52 Forms/C2118/16

Instructions regarding War Diaries and Intelligence Summaries are contained in F. S. Regs., Part II. and the Staff Manual respectively. Title pages will be prepared in manuscript.

WAR DIARY
or
~~INTELLIGENCE SUMMARY.~~
(Erase heading not required.)

Army Form C. 2118.

Place	Date	Hour	Summary of Events and Information (DADVS 18th Div. Vol 45) Sht. 4	Remarks and references to Appendices
LIGNY	31-3-19		During the month eleven horse sales were held. The demand for them in the Divisional area was not great but better prices were realised at CAMBRAI where two sales were held. There were in all 242 mules sold at the average price of 639.5 francs and 319 horses at the average price of 787 francs. 15% of these horses were a poor class of light draught. Sales of forage under 3rd Army authority No 12003/402(2D1) took place at four horse sales when 21457 Kgs of oats and 16872 Kgs of hay were disposed of. This concession was greatly appreciated by the buyers and helped to improve the prices obtained for the animals sold. The present Animal Strength of the Division is shown on attached list. All V.O.s except myself are under orders to leave the Division. The M.V.S. will be at cadre strength on April 4th.	Attd. [illegible]
			C.H. Williamson Maj. ADVS 18 D	

D. D. & L., London, E.C.
(A10266) Wt W5300/P713 750,000 2/18 Sch. 52 Forms/C2118/16

179
END

www.ingramcontent.com/pod-product-compliance
Lightning Source LLC
Chambersburg PA
CBHW081402160426
43193CB00013B/2086

* 9 7 8 1 4 7 4 5 1 0 6 6 0 *